DUBLIN'S LOST TREASURES
Vanished Places in Dublin

HUGH ORAM

Order this book online at www.trafford.com
or email orders@trafford.com

Most Trafford titles are also available at major online book retailers.

© Copyright 2019 Hugh Oram.

All rights reserved. No part of this publication may be reproduced, stored in a retrieval system, or transmitted, in any form or by any means, electronic, mechanical, photocopying, recording, or otherwise, without the written prior permission of the author.

Print information available on the last page.

isbn: 978-1-4907-9481-5 (sc)
isbn: 978-1-4907-9482-2 (hc)
isbn: 978-1-4907-9484-6 (e)

Library of Congress Control Number: 2019904553

Because of the dynamic nature of the Internet, any web addresses or links contained in this book may have changed since publication and may no longer be valid. The views expressed in this work are solely those of the author and do not necessarily reflect the views of the publisher, and the publisher hereby disclaims any responsibility for them.

Any people depicted in stock imagery provided by Getty Images are models, and such images are being used for illustrative purposes only.
Certain stock imagery © Getty Images.

Trafford rev. 04/17/2019

Trafford PUBLISHING www.trafford.com
North America & international
toll-free: 1 888 232 4444 (USA & Canada)
fax: 812 355 4082

ACKNOWLEDGEMENTS

I should especially like to thank my dear wife, Bernadette, for all her help and encouragement during my book career over the past four decades.

I'm indebted to various friends, who' ve all given me lots of encouragement during the process of writing this book, Thelma Byrne, Dublin; Christina Cannon, Dublin; Aisling Curley, Dublin; Miriam Doyle, Blackrock, Co Dublin; Maria Gillen, Athlone and Mary Murphy, Caherlistrane, near Tuam, Co Galway.

The help is much appreciated of the various Dublin newspapers that published my letter, which started the ball rolling with this book, and which generated a huge amount of replies and photographs. I also owe a great debt of gratitude to the following people who' ve helped with its compilation; they are listed in chronological order.

Michelle Clarke; Michael Doyle; Ken Finlay (Old Dublin Society) ; David Givens (The Liffey Press) ; Breda Lynch; Tara Buckley and Carmel Egan (RGDATA) ; Michael Lee; Mary Reynolds; Bernadette McPolin; Harry Havelin; Eithne McKeon; Alex Findlater; Yvonne Altman O' Connor (Jewish Museum, Dublin) ; Dr Stephanie Rains (Maynooth University; Angela O' Connell (Rathmines Historical Society); Maurice Curtis; Margaret

Pfeiffer; Des Kerins; Deirdre McParland (ESB Archives) ; Nóra Naszályi (Irish Countrywomen's Association) ; John Bryan Allen; Adrienne Bourke; Fergus McCafferty; Susan Roundtree; Mary Duffy Ryan; Martin Ryan; Kathleen Horgan.

Bróna Uí Loing; Bill McLoughlin; Liam Quinn; Joan Purcell; Bernie Ladd; Carmel and Tony Keeling; Tony and Gertrude Reynolds; Andrew Jones; Jennifer Kingston; Christy Hehir (An Post museum and archive) ; Prof Conal Hooper; Jimmy Doyle; Bridie Armstrong; Helen Farrell (Old Lucan Society) ; Neil O' Callaghan; Brian Speirs; Richard Heaney; Jim Commins; Ina Bowden; Michael Doyle; Katherine Murphy (Irish Theatre Institute) ; Máirtín Mac Con Iomaire (School of Culinary Arts and Food Technology, Technological University, Dublin); Michael Brennan, Glasnevin; Colum O' Riordan (Irish Architectural Archive) and John Holohan (Ballsbridge, Donnybrook and Sandymount Historical Society). I should also like to thank Dean Lochner of the Bondi Group, Ballsbridge, Dublin, for all his technical help and Hackett's Digital, Lower Baggot Street, Dublin, for their always efficient scanning service.

INTRODUCTION

Over the past 50 years, Dublin and its suburbs have changed immeasurably. Shopping centres, both in the city centre and in the suburbs, as well as many internationally owned shops, have transformed retailing, but part of the price of that advance has been the destruction of many old shops and other community organisations.

But the old shops and other places, and the old ways of shopping, are still fondly remembered by many people, as testified by the huge response I've had for requests for anecdotes, other material and old photographs. In the order in which they are listed in the book, I've detailed many places that have been swept away in the relentless tide of change, especially during the so- called Celtic Tiger years between 1995 and 2008, and in more recent times, since the many false idols of a boom economy started returning in 2015.

I' ve listed nightclubs, cinemas, theatres, old newspapers, restaurants and cafés, hotels, shops and department stores, buildings, shopping streets and roads, districts, organisations and businesses. The list of what we' ve lost is long and complex and while I've tried to include as many of the vanished places as possible, it's inevitable that some have been left out.

But in the contents of the book, I' ve tried to give as much description of what has been swept away in the name of progress, over the past 50 years, and what those losses have meant in terms of the city's infrastructure, its sense of social and cultural cohesion and the often very personalised service provided by those vanished shops and other places.

BALLROOMS AND NIGHTCLUBS

Bondi Beach Club

This nightclub, on Ormond Quay, was renowned for its beach-like interior and its foam parties. It lasted until 2011, close to the Unicef offices.

McGonagles, South Anne Street

McGonagles was a very trendy ballroom that had started up in the 1950s. In the 1960s, many showbands performed there, but it closed down 20 years ago and was demolished. It was replaced by a shop development occupied by Hacketts, a London- based fashion designer, which lasted there until 2014. What was once Hacketts is now occupied by Magees, the renowned Co Donegal tweed firm.

Club 92

The so- called 'Club of Love' flourished in Leopardstown for close on 30 years, but closed down in 2018.

Dandelion

This establishment on St Stephen's Green West functioned as a restaurant, a bar and a nightclub. One of its claims to fame was that it was the first bar in Ireland to serve drinks in glasses made from polished ice. A receiver was appointed in 2011.

Lillie Bordellos

A famed late night venue at the bottom of Grafton Street, it has now been replaced by Lost Lane, featuring the best in sound and lighting, where Irish and international stars can perform.

McGrattan's

McGrattans in Fitzwilliam Lane, just off Lower Baggot Street, was at Number 76, which had long history as a club and a nightclub. Between 1962 and 1975, the premises was run as The Graduate Club, for graduates of the National University of Ireland. Then it became Barbarella's night club; in 1978, Dublin writer Ulick O' Connor said it had the most naked girls in Dublin. One of the highlights was what happened at midnight every night, when one of those girls jumped into the fountain.

Barbarella's was put up for sale in 1983 and it was turned into Alexander's nightclub, which lasted until 1988. It then underwent another transformation, into McGrattan's restaurant, run by Dan McGrattan, partner of former RTÉ television newsreader Anne Doyle.

Olympic Ballroom, Pleasants Street

The Olympic Ballroom was once one of the top dancing venues in Dublin, especially during the era of the showbands during the 1960s. But it closed down at the end of the 1990s and was demolished in 2001. The development that was built on the site includes the headquarters of Alone, a leading organisation for senior citizens.

Palace nightclub

This Camden Street nightclub hung in there for 20 years. It was once the Camden Palace De Luxe, which was rebuilt in the 1970s as an hotel and entertainment complex, with the Palace nightclub on the first floor. It was put up for sale in 2016.

Parnell Square

This square was once noted for two ballrooms, the Ierne, which had started in the 1960s, and the National Ballroom. The Ierne reopened in 2007 after a 15 year hiatus, but its reopening was short lived. The National Ballroom had a much longer existence, when it was often regarded as the top dancing venue in Dublin. It closed down in 1989 after 69 years in business.

Play nightclub

This nightclub managed to keep going on an offering of cheap drinks and a large dance floor.

Renards

Renards in South Frederick Street was much more of a nightclub than a ballroom, but it too closed down 20 years ago to make way for an office development. In its heyday, the people who went to Renards considered themselves more famous than those who went to the nearby Lillie's Bordello. That nightclub opened in the early 1990s and its plush Victorian- style red velvet furnishings highlighted its decadent look. It was so upmarket that it even had a library. The place attracted many well- known people from the music industry in Ireland and abroad, but sadly, it has now closed down.

Sloopys

Sloopys nightclub in Fleet Street was a highlight of Dublin's social and dancing scene in the 1970s. It had been started in D' Olier Street in 1969, then two years later, moved to Fleet Street. Sloopys had a bar and restaurant, but it was also a great place for dancing, including its Saturday night disco specials. In 1977, it was running a Miss Sloopy contest on Monday nights; among the judges was TV and radio presenter Pat Kenny. Sloopys lasted at Numbers 71 and 72 Fleet Street until 1988.

The Wright Venue, Swords

This large, modern venue closed down in January, 2019, after 10 years, during which it attracted many high profile performers, including Rihanna. The lease was taken over by another company, which is opening another venue on the site, called The Jam Factory.

Tripod nightclub

Based in Harcourt Street, it was renowned for its circular leather seats. It closed down in 2012.

TV Club, Harcourt Street

The old TV Club at the top of Harcourt Street was owned by broadcaster Eamonn Andrews, but it too was demolished over 20 years and replaced by an office block. Before it became the TV Club, it was well- known as the Four Provinces ballroom.

Buck Whaley's, Lower Leeson Street

Buck Whaley's, at 67 Lower Leeson Street, was one of the Leeson Street strip's most renowned night clubs, from the early 1980s until 2015, when it closed down. Its replacement, the Stone Leaf bar and restaurant, started in 2017, but later that year, the premises was put up for sale. These days, the nightclub scene in Lower Leeson Street is much diminished; one of the few survivors is the Angels lap dancing club, founded in 200. The Sugar Club, in the old Irish Film Centre cinema, also continues to do well.

Zhivago's

Zhivago's nightclub opened in 1970, named after the 1965 film, Dr Zhivago. It was in Fitzwilliam Lane, just off Lower Baggot Street and had three separate dance areas, as well as a restaurant. Its advertising slogan soon made it famous; Zhivago's was promoted as "the place where love stories begin". But by the mid 1980s, the nightclub scene had begun to change and Zhivago's moved to a nearby building that fronted onto Lower Baggot Street. But by 1987, it was all over for the nightclub, when the building was turned into office space. The Sunday Tribune newspaper became a tenant and stayed until it closed down in 2011. Today, the building houses a gym, while there's a Tesco supermarket on the ground floor.

OLD CHURCHES

Blessed Sacrament chapel, D' Olier Street

This chapel was a comparatively recent arrival in D' Olier Street, opened in 1970 on the site of the old Red Bank restaurant. It proved popular with local shoppers and tourists, but only lasted 25 years until it was closed down and replaced by a similar chapel on Bachelor's Walk, which opened in 1995.

Episcopal Church, Waterloo Road

The old Episcopal church at the Upper Baggot Street end of Waterloo Road was once a fine sight, with its soaring façade. It was also very capacious and could hold a congregation of 1, 200. The church survived from the early 19th century until the early 20th century and was demolished in the early 1920s. Subsequently, the site was cleared and used for the construction of St Martin's House in the 1960s; it accommodated such organisations as the National Roads Authority, which lasted until 2015. In 2016, St Martin's House was renamed the Waterloo Exchange. Where the façade of the church once stood on Upper Baggot Street, there are two very different retail outlets, Eddie Rocket's Diner and Helga Schworer's ladies' hairdressing salon.

Methodist church, St Stephen's Green

Methodists once had a magnificent church on the southside of St Stephen's Green, a building with a colonnaded façade that dated from the earlier 19th century. It was destroyed by a fire in 1968 that ravaged the interior. The building was never restored as a church and the Methodists moved their services to Christ Church in Leeson Park. From the late 1970s, the Methodists shared this church for nearly 30 years with the Church of Ireland. As for the church on St Stephen's Green, it was eventually restored and now houses the Department of Justice and Equality.

St Andrew's Church, St Andrew Street

The present St Andrew's Church of Ireland church in St Andrew Street dates from 1862, but there had been previous churches on this site since Viking times, around 1, 200 years ago. An earlier church had been the chapel for the nearby Irish Houses of Parliament in the 18th century, but this building was replaced by another church in 1800, and it was the destruction of this church by fire in 1860 that led to the present building being constructed. The church with its striking spire has long since passed out of religious use; for the past 20 years, until recently, it was used as a tourist information office, but it's now due to get brand new uses, as a food emporium, banqueting hall and cultural centre.

OLD CINEMAS

Adelphi, Middle Abbey Street

The Adelphi cinema had already become very popular in the 1930s, when a second screen was added in January, 1939. It was here that the Beatles made their only Irish appearance, on November 8, 1963. In the 1970s, various changes were made, giving it four screens, but it closed for the last time in 1995 and four years later, was demolished. The Dublin area had another Adelphi cinema, this one in Upper George's Street, Dún Laoghaire, which lasted from 1947 until 1971. It was eventually demolished.

Astor, Eden Quay

The Astor was Dublin's first arthouse cinema, opened in 1953, although it was in the shadow of the much larger neighbouring cinema, the Corinthian. The Astor managed to survive until 1984; it was subsequently demolished. The Corinthian had opened much earlier, in 1921 and managed to last longer, not closing until 1993. It too was subsequently demolished.

Cabra Grand

The Cabra Grand was a vast single screen cinema, that opened in 1949. It could seat 1, 650 patrons and changed its programmes three times a week during the 1950s. But it was one of the first casualties of the Irish television service that had opened in 1962; the Cabra Grand closed in 1970 after just 21 years in business and was converted into a bingo hall, with some retail outlets.

Carlton, Upper O'Connell Street

The Carlton was built on the site of a previous cinema in Upper O' Connell Street and opened in 1938, complete with its own restaurant. It ended up with a total of four screens. During the 1970s, many famous performers came to the Carlton to put on live shows, including Johnny Cash, Marlene Dietrich, Fats Domino and Duke Ellington. The cinema closed in 1994 and the site is likely to be include in a huge development mooted for this part of O' Connell Street and stretching as far as Moore Street and Parnell Street. It's scheduled to be completed by 2022. The nearby cinema at the start of Parnell Square, which went under various names such as the Rotunda and the Ambassador, lasted from 1910 until 1999, although the building continued to be used for many entertainment events.

Casino, Finglas

The Casino in Glasnevin Avenue, Finglas, had a remarkable short lifespan as a single screen cinema, lasting from 1955 until 1972. After it was closed, it was taken over by the old Superquinn company for use as a supermarket.

Classic, Terenure

The Classic was opened in 1938 with the latest in cinema technology; it lasted until 1976, when it closed down. The old cinema was converted into the Terenure Enterprise Centre with close on 30 small businesses. Just across the road from the Classic was another media mainstay of Terenure, the Sunday World offices, which are now located in Talbot Street in the city centre.

Curzon, Middle Abbey Street

When the Curzon opened in 1968, it was one of the last of the new cinemas in Dublin during that decade. The Curzon was renamed the Lighthouse in 1989, which specialised in arthouse and foreign films. It managed to last until 1996 and the building was subsequently demolished. However, the Lighthouse name continues in the modern cinema complex in Smithfield.

Dorset Picture House, Granby Row

Opened in 1911, it went through several changes of format, including being renamed the Plaza in 1928. In 1967, after a major makeover, it reopened as the Plaza Cinerama, showing the wide format films that had started to become popular in the late 1950s. It managed to last until it closed in 1981; the building was then converted into a wax museum, which lasted until 2005, when the building was demolished for a hotel development.

Drumcondra Grand

The Drumcondra Grand, often known locally as 'The Drummer', was opened in palatial style in 1934 as the first cinema in the city specifically designed for sound films. It managed to last until 1968 and is now a Tesco supermarket.

Eblana cinema, Busárus

The small basement cinema opened in 1953, when Busáras, the brand new central bus station, opened. The cinema, which could only hold 150 patrons, showed newsreels for many years, until it started screening arthouse films in the 1970s. It managed to survive until 1975, when it was turned into a theatre, which lasted for another 20 years.

Fairview Grand

The Fairview Grand opened on the main street at Marino in 1929 and in time, it was turned into a two screen cinema. The last part of the cinema closed in 1974 and subsequently, in 2005, part of the auditorium was demolished to make way for an apartment development. For a time, the old cinema was used as a preview cinema, but other uses included as the headquarters of a short-lived Dublin newspaper at the start of the 21st century. In 2006, the lobby area of the old cinema was turned into a small supermarket.

Film Centre, Burgh Quay

This small cinema operated from 1966 until 1984 on the ground floor of O' Connell Bridge House, at the corner of Burgh Quay and D' Olier Street.

Gala cinema, Ballyfermot

The Gala, which had a huge auditorium, opened on Ballyfermot Road in 1955; it was the second largest suburban cinema in Dublin, the largest being the Casino at Finglas. For its first decade, the Gala remained popular, despite the advent of television. It also became renowned for its two ushers, one of whom was nicknamed 'Harry the Hippo' because of his size. The Gala closed down in 1980 and was subsequently used for such purposes as a bingo hall and snooker hall.

Grafton newsreel cinema, Grafton Street

This newsreel cinema, close to Bewley's and on the same side of the street, opened in 1911 and closed in 1973; it became a newsreel cinema in 1959, specialising in newsreels and cartoons. It closed down in 1973 and the premises was converted into a shop for a fashion retailer.

Green cinema, St Stephen's Green

The Green cinema, on the west side of St Stephen's Green, close to the College of Surgeons, began life in 1937. For a time late in its existence, it was used as the Irish Film Centre, and lasted until 1987. The cinema was then demolished, one of many buildings demolished on that side of the Green and in South King Street, to make way for the St Stephen's Green shopping centre, which opened in 1988. A new multi- screen cinema was due to be built as part of the new shopping centre, but that particular plan never materialised.

Inchicore cinema, Tyrconnell Road

The Inchicore cinema opened in 1921 and was expanded in 1943. In 1973, it was renamed the Europa, then three years later, it was given another new name, the Pullman Studio. It closed down in 1980 and was demolished.

Irish Film Censor's office, Harcourt Terrace

For many years, the Film Censor's office in Harcourt Terrace had an unenviable record for cutting films or either banning them altogether. Between the 1920s and the 1980s, over 2, 500 films were banned in Ireland, while over 11, 000 films were cut.

The Film Censor's office was built in 1943 and timber was in such short supply during the second world war, the rafters were made from concrete. One of the last film censors was TV personality Frank Hall, who worked in the role between 1978 and 1986. He applied the censorship rules very strictly, in an effort to preserve family values. The job came after the great success he had in the 1960s and early 1970s with his satirical programme on RTÉ, Hall's Pictorial Weekly. Yet despite his efforts at preserving family values, he had a long running affair with a young colleague in RTÉ, while he also had an even longer running affair with agony aunt Frankie Byrne, with whom he had a daughter.

Irish Film Theatre, Earlsfort Terrace

The cinema on the ground floor of the Irish Sugar Company building on Earlsfort Terrace opened in 1963 as a private cinema, lasting as such until 1976. In 1977, it reopened as the Irish Film Theatre and under that name, lasted until 1985. It remained disused for 14 years, until it became the Sugar Club, still operating today, and which has its entrance in Lower Leeson Street. The Irish Film Centre opened at Eustace Street in Temple Bar in 1992 and is still functioning today.

Kenilworth, Harold's Cross

Also known as the Classic 2 in the years before it closed, it shut in 2003 and the cinema was eventually demolished. In 2018, the site was put up for sale and there was much speculation that a large development of apartments could be built there.

Killester cinema

The Killester cinema opened as a modern style cinema with a large auditorium in 1943 and lasted until 1970. The building was then converted to office use.

Landscape cinema, Churchtown

The Landscape cinema took its name from its location on Landscape Road; it opened in 1955, at a time when new suburban cinemas were still being opened. But the lifespan of this single screen cinema was short, a mere decade. It closed in 1965 and the building was converted into offices.

Leinster, Dolphin's Barn

The Leinster cinema opened at Dolphin's Barn in 1936, just two days in advance of the rival Rialto cinema, close by. During its years as a cinema, it had a couple of shops, which included first a tailors, then a butchers and finally a shoe repairers. The neighbouring Rialto cinema closed in 1968 and was converted into a car showrooms, while the Leinster closed soon afterwards. The old Leinster cinema became an ice skating venue for several years, but after that closed, the building was demolished in 2004.

Manor Street Picture House

One of the first cinemas to open in Dublin, in 1914, its name was subsequently changed twice, first to the Palladium, then the Broadway. After it closed in 1956, it was used by a cooperage company, then in 1988, it became a community resource centre.

Mary Street Picture House

This cinema opened in 1912 and despite being a fleapit cinema, like the old Princess in Rathmines, it managed to keep going until 1959. Noted for its architectural extravagances, the building became the headquarters of the old PMPA insurance company and is today occupied by the Axa insurance company, part of AIB.

Metropole, O' Connell Street

The Metropole cinema, facing a side of the GPO, was constructed in 1922. The hotel and restaurant that had previously occupied the site had been destroyed during the Easter Week 1916 shelling in what was then Sackville Street, now O' Connell Street. This large cinema lasted until 1972, as did the restaurant and ballroom at the front of the building, facing onto O' Connell Street. In 1973, the whole complex was demolished and a large department store built on the site, for British Home Stores. It lasted there until 1992, when the building was taken over by Penney' s, still trading there today.

Odeon, Dundrum Road

This cinema opened in 1944, with parking for 500 bicycles. Between screening films, the Odeon was also used for live variety shows, which lasted until the 1960s. The cinema closed down in 1967 and the building was subsequently converted into the Apollo Building, containing the offices of several companies.

Ormonde cinema, Stillorgan

The original Ormonde cinema opened in 1954 and survived until 1978. The building was demolished to make way for a shopping complex and a new cinema, also called the Ormonde, which opened in 1983 and continues to operate as a multiplex.

Ritz, Serpentine Avenue, Sandymount

Originally opened as the Astoria, in 1936, it changed its name in 1947 to the Ritz, then in 1976, was turned into the Oscar Theatre, which managed to survive until 1976. It subsequently became Dublin's first Sikh temple.

Sandford cinema, Ranelagh

This cinema, on Sandford Road, opened in 1914. Then, in the 1930s, its name was changed to Sandford Green. The cinema closed in 1978 and the building subsequently included Wong's Chinese restaurant, as well as offices. In January, 2013, the building was badly damaged by fire, but has now been restored.

Screen, Hawkins Street

The Screen cinema, opened in 1972 as a single screen cinema, became a popular venue for movie fans. The cinema had a small bronze statue outside of a cinema usher. It closed down in early 2016 and was demolished in 2018 to make way for a large office development. Earlier, from 1962 onwards, the cinema on this site had traded as the Regal, becoming the New Metropole for a brief time.

State cinema, Phibsboro'

The State cinema on the North Circular Road, Phibsboro', opened in 1954 and lasted until 1981; during the last few years of its existence, it had been used for screenings by the Irish Film

Society. After it closed, it had other uses, including as an ice rink (until 2000) and as a carpet showrooms.

Stella cinema, Rathmines

When this cinema opened in 1923, it was the largest in Dublin, far more upmarket than the other cinema in Rathmines, the Princess. The Stella was converted into a twin cinema in 1981, but this failed to stop its decline. Three generations of the O' Grady family had run it until they sold the cinema to the Ward Anderson group in 2003. The new owners closed it down until 2004, but it reopened as the most luxurious cinema in Dublin, in 2017.

A second cinema had the same name, the Stella in Mount Merrion, which opened in 1955 and even had a ballroom next door. The cinema lasted for 21 years, until 1976, when it closed down and was converted into furniture showrooms. These were demolished in February, 2019, to make way for an apartment development.

Sutton Grand

The Sutton Grand opened in 1937 as a modern style cinema; it lasted 1967, after which the ground floor was converted to a Superquinn supermarket.

The Cinema, Chapelizod

Opened in 1942, it underwent two name changes, first to the Majestic, then the Oriel. It survived until 1966, when television was causing a dramatic decline in cinema audiences. The building was subsequently turned into a factory for a company called ML Manufacturing, but by 2006, the building had been abandoned.

Tower cinema, Clondalkin

This cinema, on Clondalkin's Main Street, opened in 1939, the building converted from a bus garage. The cinema, with a small auditorium, was given the nickname of 'The Bivvo' by local people. Yet the cinema managed to change its programmes four times a week, more than was the case with most other Dublin cinemas. It was extended in 1957 to include Cinemascope screening equipment, but it finally closed in 1977 and was converted to retail use.

Whitehall Grand

This cinema opened in 1954 and lasted for a mere 20 years, until 1974. It was then taken over for use as a bingo hall.

OLD HOSPITALS

Baggot Street hospital

Once known as the Royal City of Dublin Hospital, in Upper Baggot Street, it was opened in 1832 and was enlarged in 1895. It is still used by the HSE for the provision of medical and social care services, but in 2019, it announced that it was going to make another attempt to sell off the building to a developer. If the sale goes ahead, it's likely the building, with its distinctive façade, will become a boutique hotel. But the HSE has stipulated that whoever develops the site will have to provide brand new medical facilities on the Haddington Road end of the site. The old nurses home, at the back of the hospital, is now the luxurious Dylan Hotel.

Mercer's Hospital

This hospital was founded in 1734 on the site of the early 13th century St Stephen's leper asylum, but it closed down in 1983. Later that decade, the St Stephen's Green shopping centre was built on an immediately adjacent site. The old hospital was converted into a medical centre for the Royal College of Surgeons of Ireland, during the 1990s.

Sir Patrick Dun's hospital

Founded in 1788, it moved to Grand Canal Street in 1808 and lasted there until its closure in 1986. The building now houses the Dublin registry office. At one stage, most of Dublin's hospitals were clustered in the city centre, but with the development of new hospitals outside the city centre, such as Beaumont, St Vincent's and Tallaght, only three are left close to the city centre. Two of those are maternity hospitals, Holles Street and the Rotunda. Holles Street hospital is due to be relocated on the St Vincent's hospital site. The Dental Hospital is still in Lincoln Place, where it has been since 1895.

Jervis Street shopping centre

This opened in 1996, on the site of the old Jervis Street Hospital, which had been founded in 1718. Once, all Dublin's hospitals were clustered in the city centre, but all have long since closed down, including Mercer's (1734), the Meath Hospital (1753), Dr Steeven's Hospital (1733), St Vincent's Hospital on St Stephen's Green (1834), and the Adelaide Hospital (1839). The old Children's Hospital at 87 and 88 Harcourt Street, dating back to 1821, was the first children's hospital in these islands and the second in Europe. In 1998, it moved to the new Tallaght Hospital, together with the Adelaide and the Meath Hospitals. St Vincent's moved to its new site in Elm Park in 1970, while the old Sir Patrick Duns became the setting for the Dublin registry office. The old Adelaide Hospital was turned into apartments.

OLD NEWSPAPERS

Dublin Evening Mail

Until 1962, when the Evening Mail closed, Dublin had three evening newspapers. Now, it has one former evening newspaper that has now been converted into an all day publication, The Herald, once the broadsheet Evening Herald.

The Evening Mail had traded for close on 140 years and was based at the top of Parliament Street. Widely regarded as a Protestant newspaper, it was noted for its jottings and its readers' letters.

Evening News

After the Irish Press group closed down in 1995, some of its former employees started a new evening newspaper in Dublin, the Evening News, which started in May, 1996. It had over 60 employees, from the former Irish Press group. The new paper cost £1. 5 million to launch; the main shareholder was the Midland Tribune group in Birr, Co Offaly. The new newspaper was based in Donnybrook, Dublin, and used new technology to send the made up pages direct to the printers, in Birr and in Ashbourne, Co Meath. The circulation target was 35, 000 but the initial optimism was short lived; the new newspaper collapsed after just four months.

Irish Press group

The Irish Press group closed down in 1995 after trading for over 60 years. It had started in 1931 with a single newspaper, the morning Irish Press, controlled by the de Valera family. Éamon de Valera had founded the Fianna Fáil party in 1926; he subsequently became a long serving Taoiseach, then President of Ireland. The Sunday Press was founded in 1949 and went on to become a huge seller, with a circulation at its height of 400, 000. The third newspaper in the group was the Evening Press, started in 1954 with Douglas Gageby as editor. He went on to become editor of The Irish Times. At its height, the Evening Press was also hugely successful, selling 175, 000 copies a night. But by the later 1980s, the newspaper group was floundering and its demise came as little surprise.

Metro Herald freesheet

The Evening Herald started a freesheet called Herald AM, while the international Metro freesheet launched in Ireland as Metro Ireland. But both found the market for advertising increasingly difficult and they merged their operations in 2010. However, the merged freesheet only managed to keep going until 2014, when it closed down in the face of continuing losses. The on the street distribution of first the two freesheets, then the merged title, became a familiar part of Dublin life, especially with morning commuters.

Sunday Tribune

For many years, the Sunday Tribune was the only Irish Sunday newspaper that had a radical slant to its content, especially when Vincent Browne was the editor. But the unsuccessful launch of a Dublin freesheet undermined the finances of the Sunday Tribune, which was eventually absorbed into Independent News & Media. It closed down for the last time in 2011.

OLD OFFICES

Former Bord Fáilte offices

Old offices are rarely mourned, but one exception was just by Baggot Street Bridge, the old offices of Bord Fáilte, defunct for a decade now. These offices were designed by Robin Walker of Michael Scott & Partners and completed in 1962 at a cost of £50,000. They were regarded as a good example of Irish modernist architecture in the 1960s, but despite many calls for their preservation, they were demolished in late 2018.

Old newspaper offices

Dublin once had a fine selection of old newspaper offices, notably The Irish Times and Independent News & Media.

The Irish Times occupied a vintage building, between Westmoreland Street and D' Olier Street, with its works entrance in Fleet Street, for well over a century. The building had many offices on different levels, until a large scale newsroom was constructed within its confines. The old building had great character and characters, but in 2006, the newspaper moved to brand new offices in nearby Tara Street.

Independent News & Media used to be based in a 1920s building in Middle Abbey Street, that like The Irish Times building, was characterised by an endless variety of corridors. Both The Irish Times and Independent News & Media used to print their newspapers in their headquarters buildings, but both relocated their printing to Citywest, on the outskirts of the city. Independent News & Media moved two years before The Irish Times, in 2004, to new offices in Talbot Street.

The Irish Daily Star, launched in 1988, used to have offices well outside the city centre, first at Terenure then in Dundrum, but eventually, it too moved to Talbot Street. The Sunday World occupied offices that had once been the Terenure Laundry, but it too moved to Talbot Street; its Terenure site was sold in 2005.

Another comparatively recent newspaper, the Sunday Business Post, occupied various locations over the years, including Merchant's Quay, Lower Pembroke Street and currently, the Merrion Centre.

A long vanished newspaper company, the Irish Press group, which published the Irish Press morning newspaper, the Evening Press evening newspaper and the Sunday Press, closed down in 1995. Founded in 1931, it had occupied the site of the old Tivoli Theatre on Burgh Quay and its offices were characterised by its large newsroom and a succession of offices. After the group closed down, its offices were demolished and replaced by new offices for the Irish Naturalisation and Immigration Office.

OLD RESTAURANTS, HOTELS AND PUBS

Alfredo' s, Mary's Abbey

Alfredo's restaurant, at Number 14 Mary's Abbey, just off Capel Street, was the place to go during the 1960s for celebrity dining and dancing; it had been founded in 1953.

An Béal Bocht, Charlemont Street

Named after the novel by Myles na Gopaleen, this pub was famous for its rousing sessions. Popular belief had it that it was owned by the Black family, of whom renowned singer Mary Black is a member, but it was owned and run by Carmel Gleeson and her son, Mick. The pub was demolished around 30 years ago.

The Aviary

This pub was once the only building in Dublin's shortest street, Canon Street, just off Bride Street and close to St Patrick's Cathedral. The Aviary had birds in cages in its interior, while for many years, the Dublin Bird Market took place in an alleyway at the back of the pub. The other part of Canon Street had been incorporated into St Patrick's Park in 1904, but The Aviary pub was demolished and Canon Street was incorporated into a widening of Bride Street in 1963.

Belgard Inn, Tallaght

The Belgard Inn closed down in March, 2018, after more than 40 years in existence. A new Lidl supermarket was planned for the site.

Bernardo's, Lincoln Place

Bernardo's was started by the Gentile family in 1954 and its location, at the back of Trinity College, proved popular for many years with journalists, writers, music and theatre people. It became the longest running Italian restaurant in Dublin and also spawned the old Quo Vadis restaurant in St Andrew Street. Bernado's closed in 2000 and the man who did so much to keep it going and after whom it was named, Bernado Gentile, died in 2011 at the age of 91.

Big Tree pub, Drumcondra

This pub, on the main road in Drumcondra, and close to Croke Park, was a favourite with GAA match goers for decades, but it closed down in 2018. The site is due to be developed as an hotel.

Coffee Inn, South Anne Street

The Italian- run Coffee Inn ran from 1954 until 1995 and was a popular place, especially during the 1970s and 1980s, for students and musicians. For the late, great Phil Lynott, it was a favourite spot.

Coq Hardi, Pembroke Road

This upmarket restaurant was started by John Howard and his wife in 1977, in a Georgian style house at the corner of Pembroke Road and Wellington Road, Ballsbridge. One of the frequent diners there was Charles Haughey, a former Taoiseach. On one occasion, he brought his entire cabinet for dinner there. Haughey chose beef for his main course and when the waiter asked him what vegetables he'd like, Haughey replied: "they' ll have the same". Haughey also frequently brought his mistress, the late Terry Keane, a social diarist with the Sunday Independent, to dine in the Coq Hardi, thus producing a blizzard of legendary stories, most of which were untrue.

Empire Bar, Swords

For decades, the Empire Bar in Swords, north Co Dublin, was a popular pub of choice for locals, but it went into liquidation in August, 2018, and closed down. It reopened, in November, 2018, as The Betsy.

Expresso restaurant, St Mary's Road

The old Expresso restaurant in St Mary's Road, just off Upper Baggot Street in Ballsbridge, was run by Ann- Marie Nohl. Over the years, it became a hangout for many well- known people and stories generated there kept the social diairies of the Sunday

Independent and other newspapers well supplied with gossip. It was commonplace to see such celebrities as Louis Walsh, Daniel Day Lewis and Van Morrison dining there, but this high flying social venue came to an abrupt end in 2013 when the Expresso restaurant went into liquidation.

It then did a quick transformation into Marcel's Restaurant, but in 2016, it assumed its current use, as a luxury beauty salon trading under the name of Callan & Co.

The Forest Lounge

This once popular bar once came to prominence in the mid-1990s, as a popular spot for LGBT customers. It closed down in 2015 and was replaced by Street 66, renowned for its live reggae and ska music.

Golden Orient, Lower Leeson Street

This remarkable Indian restaurant was started at 27 Lower Leeson Street in 1956 by Mohammed 'Mike' Butt, a Kenyan of Kashmiri descent, and his Dublin- born wife, Terry, a graduate of the Cathal Brugha Street college of catering. It became so popular, so quickly, that by 1973, Dublin had nine other Indian restaurants, all trying to emulate the success of the Golden Orient. By 1980, Mike Butt was sharing the work load in the restaurant with two other people, but eventually, because of his own ill health and a severe downturn in the economy, the restaurant closed down in 1984. Mike Butt died in 1988.

Grafton Lounge

Situated on the Royal Hibernian Way, this bar and restaurant was renamed in 2016 as Lemon & Duke.

Groome's Hotel, Parnell Square

For many years, Groome's Hotel was the place to go in the city centre for late night drinking well into the early hours. Joseph

Groome, who founded the hotel, was a founding member of Fianna Fáil and hardly surprisingly, it became a hangout for many politicians from that party as well as for members of the Labour Party. Newspaper workers, painters, poets, writers and other celebrities also supped there, but essentially, Groome's was known as a sub- office of the Dáil. It closed down in 1973 and converted into offices, but in the late 1990s, the building was redeveloped as Cassidy's Hotel. In homage to the old hotel, Cassidy's now has Groome's bar and bistro.

Another famed all- night drinking place was The Irish Times Club in Fleet Street, which opened up at midnight for workers from that newspaper and remained open until 6. 30 am.

Hourican's pub in Lower Leeson Street

Was a small, traditional and very cosy pub, a good place for a pint and a toastie. It was often used by diplomats from the nearby Department of Foreign Affairs and Trade. It was run by Pat and Mary Hourican for 38 years until it was closed down in 2016 on their retirement. However, in early 2019, the boarded up front was renovated in preparation for a planned reopening.

Jammet's, Nassau Street

Jammet's restaurant used to be the 'in' place to dine in Dublin, frequented by many local and visiting celebrities until it closed in 1967. Michael and Francois Jammet, from south- west France, had bought the Burlington restaurant and oyster room in St Andrew Street in 1900 and in 1901, reopened it as Jammet' s. It remained there until the lease expired in 1926, when they moved to Nassau Street. After the restaurant closed, the premises eventually became the Berni Inn; the contrast between its menus and those of the old Jammets couldn't have been greater.

Jurys Hotel, Dame Street

The old Jury's Hotel in Dame Street traced its origins back to an inn on College Green set up in 1839 by William Jury, a former commercial traveller. The hotel itself was built in the 1850s, a very solid looking building that contained good facilities for guests. The hotel survived until 1973; the building was demolished in 1980. But one element of the hotel was saved, the ornate bar, which was taken down and reassembled in an hotel in Zurich.

The Intercontinental Hotel in Ballsbridge- not to be confused with the present day Intercontinental Hotel in Ballsbridge, was opened in 1963 and when Jury's in Dame Street closed, that hotel moved to Ballsbridge and the Intercontinental was renamed Jury's Hotel. These days, it's known as the Ballsbridge Hotel, but it is due to demolished and replaced by an apartment development within the next couple of years.

Kiely' s, Donnybrook

For many years, from the early 1960s onwards, Kiely's was a favourite place for off duty RTÉ staff. It had an art gallery on the first floor and it was often said that Kiely's was that rare place in Dublin where art was above drink. Kiely's closed down in 1982; an adjacent pub, Madigan' s, on the corner of Belmont Avenue and

Morehampton Road, was also a popular venue for RTÉ personnel, but it closed down earlier and was converted into a restaurant. The site of McCloskey's pub, close to the Donnybrook Fair supermarket, is due to be redeveloped into apartments, which will leave Donnybrook with just one pub, Maynes, a reincarnation of the old Long's pub.

Kilmartin's, Upper Baggot Street

This bistro style restaurant traded from 1979 until 1993, run by husband and wife team Alan Aitchison and his wife Patricia, who now works for the Trocadero restaurant in the city centre. The restaurant was named after Kilmartin's bookie's shop that had previously stood on the site. The restaurant was very popular with locals as well as visitors to Ireland and also attracted a lot of high profile diners, such as the late Bernadette Greevy, the singer.

Nico' s, Dame Street

Nico's was a traditional style Italian restaurant started at 53 Dame Street in 1968. It was owned and run for many years by Emelio Cirillo. With its unique Irish- Italian ambience, it managed to survive until the autumn of 2018, when it closed its doors for the last time.

Palm Grove café, Grafton Street

The Italian run Palm Grove café, at Number 74 Grafton Street, was a popular place to hang out during the 1960s, as was Robert Roberts café, also at the top of Grafton Street.

Playwright pub, Blackrock

The Playwright pub, at the corner of Newtownpark Avenue and Newtown Park in Blackrock, proved a short lived venture that attracted big money; in 2004, the pub was sold for just over €8 million. After the pub closed, it was turned into a branch of the TGI Friday restaurant chain, but that branch closed too in 2011. The long vacant premises are being turned into a branch of Dunnes Stores.

Quo Vadis

This restaurant ran from 1960 until 1991 at 15 St Andrew Street and was succeed by Quo Vadis 2. During the 1970s and 1980s, it was owned and run by Cyril McCormack, son of Count John McCormack, the famous tenor. Cyril McCormack also had an interest in a restaurant on St Stephen's Green that is now the Cliff House. Cyril McCormack died in 1990, aged 83.

Ranelagh

In Ranelagh, as in most other areas of Dublin, there were only takeaways, previously known as chippers, until the 1980s, when restaurants started to develop. Ranelagh had the Pronto Grill, which became TriBeCa, the Paradise Grill and Morelli's chip shop which became Antica Venezia in 1998. Luigi's was a long running restaurant and takeaway in Ranelagh but at the end of 2019, the premises were up for sale.

Not far away from Ranelagh was Cafolla's chipper on Mespil Road, which traded from the late 1930s until 2006, when the family sold the place for €2. 7 million. After it was sold, the shop was converted into a more modern fish and chip shop, run by Beshoff Bros. Also on the southside, Borza's renowned chipper on Sandymount Green closed in 2018 after trading for close on 50 years.

Red Bank, D' Olier Street

The Red Bank restaurant was originally known as Burton Bindon's, after the oyster beds in Co Clare owned by Bindon. At the start of the 20th century, it was taken over by the Hamilton family. By 1934, it had a ground floor grill room and bar, with two further upstairs floors of dining rooms. It served some of the best restaurant food in Dublin, including its famous oysters, and was also well- known for the number of local and visiting celebrities who got spectacularly drunk there. It declined during the second world war and closed down in 1948, but was reopened under new management. It also managed to survive a fire in 1961 that gutted the place, necessitating a complete rebuild. It finally closed down in 1969 and the premises made an unlikely transition into a chapel.

Rice's Bar, corner of St Stephen's Green and South King Street

This pub had a reputation for being the first gay- friendly pub in Dublin, indeed in Ireland, but it was subsequently joined by another nearby venue, Bartley Dunnes pub on Stephen's Street Lower, near the old Mercer's Hospital. In Bartley Dunnes, a favourite trick was to glue a penny to the floor. When an unsuspecting male customer came in, spotted the penny and bent down to pick it up, he would leave himself open to assault on his rear quarters. Bartley Dunnes was replaced by Break for the Border, a super pub with five bars, three dance floors and a nightclub. Rice's closed in 1986 and was demolished to make way for the St Stephen's Green shopping centre.

Royal Hibernian Hotel

The Royal Hibernian Hotel was started in 1751, Ireland's first hotel. In 1939, it was bought by Paul Besson, who had been brought in as hotel manager in 1905. When Paul Besson died in 1950, his son Ken took over. In 1954, Hector Fabron took over as manager, later moving to the Russell Hotel. The Royal Hibernian was noted for its restaurant and bar facilities, including the three roomed La Rotisserie restaurant, opened in 1970. The hotel closed down in 1982 and the building, noted for its elegant façade, was demolished, to be replaced by a dull office block and the Royal Hibernian Way shopping mall.

Russell Hotel, St Stephen's Green

The Russell Hotel was an elegant building at the corner of St Stephen's Green and Harcourt Street; it dated from the 1880s. After the Besson family took it over- they also owned the Royal Hibernian Hotel in nearby Dawson Street- the hotel became noted for its haute cuisine. A number of well- known chefs worked there, including Pierre Rolland, Ireland's first Michelin starred chef. But the hotel closed down in 1974 and was replaced by a bleak, uninspiring office block that still stands on the site. Despite the fact that many government ministers used to dine at the Russell, none of them made any effort to save the hotel.

Soup Bowl, Molesworth Place

Run by Norma Smurfit, it had its heyday in the 1980s, when it was one of top dining out spots in Dublin city centre. One of its staff was Biddy White Lennon, who went on to become a well-known actor. It had started in the late 1960s, under the ownership of Peter Pourrie.

Swiss Chalet, Merrion Row

The Swiss Chalet was a café and bakery at Numbers 2 and 3, Merrion Row, that traded during the 1940s and 1950s. It then closed down and was boarded up for many years before it was finally demolished in 1977. A Spar supermarket now stands on the site.

The Barge

This was a floating pub that was launched on the Grand Canal in the late 1980s. Due to a loophole in the law, if it sailed on the canal, it could serve drink all night. But there was always someone on duty on the canal bank, ready to cast off the ropes and set sail if any gardaí came in sight. The inside of the floating pub was spartan and the bar area could cater for up to 30 patrons. The Barge was closed down in 1990 when the legal loophole it had exploited was closed.

The Country Shop

The Country Shop was a very popular restaurant for many years on the Shelbourne Hotel side of St Stephen's Green. It had been opened in 1930 as an outlet for women to sell surplus produce from their farms, while it was also noted for selling Irish crafts. The mainstay behind The Country Shop for many years was Muriel Gahan, who had been brought up in Co Mayo. In 1927, she had begun working with an all- women decorating company, The Modern Decorator, based in South Anne Street.

But Muriel had also become very involved with the United Irish Women's Society, started in 1910 to promote co- operation among rural women and promote craftsmanship; subsequently renamed the United Irishwomen, it was the forerunner of the Irish Countrywomen's Association, which began in 1935. But in 1930, Muriel had spotted the basement at 23, St Stephen's Green for rent; it took a dozen years for The Country Shop to find its feet, but eventually, it became a very popular restaurant, renowned for cheap and dainty food, as well as its promotion of Irish- made crafts. Among its many regulars was the writer Patrick Kavanagh.

But in 1968, the traffic flow round St Stephen's Green was reorganised and buses could no longer stop outside The Country Shop, while customers with cars had great trouble finding somewhere to park. Another blow came that year when civil servants were put on a five day week and no longer had to work on Saturday mornings. Their lunch breaks were cut from 90 minutes to one hour. A decade later, when many of the women working in The Country Shop were well past retirement age, it was decided to close the shop, with its unique street sign of a miniature thatched cottage. It shut down in September, 1978.

Muriel Gahan was very involved elsewhere; she was the only female founding member of the Arts Council and the first female vice-president of the RDS, among many other accolades. She died in St Mary's nursing home in Pembroke Park in 1995 in her 98th year.

The Long Stone pub

The Long Stone pub in Townsend Street in the city centre closed its doors for the last time in December, 2018. The interior of the pub was noted for its wall hangings. Founded in 1754, it was one of Dublin's oldest pubs and it closed down to make way for an 11 storey office development centred on Tara Street.

OLD SHOPS

Aer Lingus travel shops

In the old days, people went to a travel agent or an airline travel shop to buy their air tickets; these days, it's nearly all done online. Aer Lingus decided, in 2001, to close all its travel shops in Ireland; these included one in Upper O' Connell Street, another at the corner of Dawson Street and St Stephen's Green and a third at George's Street, Dún Laoghaire. The shop at the top of Dawson Street became a branch of Elvery's sports store, which lasted there until 2018.

À la Française, Wicklow Street, Stillorgan shopping centre and Killiney

When the Stillorgan Shopping Centre opened in 1966 as Ireland's first shopping centre, one of the shops that started up was À la Française, a delicatessen shop, owned by run by Irene McGee and her French husband, René Riou. Their French style deli items were so popular that they owned two more branches, one in Killiney, the other in Wicklow Street. Eventually, 40 years later, the shops closed down as the couple decided to retire and go and live in France.

Ballsbridge

One of the features of Ballsbridge "village" on the Merrion Road was the chemist's shop run by Hayes, Conyngham & Robinson, a long established chain that had started at Number 12 Grafton Street in 1897. Its Ballsbridge shop opened soon afterwards, in September that year. For many years, it had a delivery boy with a bicycle, who would deliver orders to customers living in the district. A distinctive feature of the shop was the large panel on its side wall that simply gave the name of the firm; it had been an advertisement panel on one of the old Dublin trams.

The chemist's shop closed down in April, 1988, and the premises were demolished to make way for Roly's restaurant, which opened in 1992. Roly's has been going strong ever since, including the more recently opened Roly's Bistro. Next door to Roly' s, on the first floor, is the Lobster Pot restaurant, which has been going since 1980.

Next door to Roly's for many years was the Bon Espresso newsagent and fast food shop; a newsagency has long featured on this site and before it became the Bon Espresso, it was The Alcove, selling both sweets and newspapers. Within the past two years, the Bon Espresso has been replaced by a food takeaway.

Ballymun

This new suburb, started with such high hopes on Dublin's northside in the 1960s, featured the Ballymun Shopping Centre, which lasted for 40 years. The last remaining tenants left what had become a very rundown shopping centre in the summer of 2018, after which Dublin City Council planned to demolish the whole shopping centre and relocate the remaining shops elsewhere. An independent Ballymun based councillor, Noeleen O' Reilly, said the demolition represented an opportunity to revitalise the town centre and bring new shops into the area. The old delapidated shopping centre was a reminder of everything that went wrong with the regeneration of the area, she added. Among those new shops is a Lidl supermarket.

Beaumont Road

This road, on Dublin's northside, had two food shops in the late 1960s, James Duff, who ran the Beaumont Stores at Number 21, selling groceries, fruit and vegetables. The address now houses a funeral directors. At Number 72, the Fairview Egg Stores went on to be replaced by Beaumont drive- in greengrocers.

Bewleys, Westmoreland Street and South Great George's Street

Bewleys had several shops and cafés in central Dublin; the sole survivor is the magnificently restored Bewleys in Grafton Street. The firm had opened a shop in South Great George's Street in 1870; a café was also opened there in 1894. This outlet lasted until 1999. In 1896, the firm opened a far larger shop and café in Westmoreland Street and that kept going until 2004, when it closed down.

The firm also expanded into the suburbs. It opened a café on the first floor of the Stillorgan shopping centre in 1970 and that lasted until 1996. Today, what was once Bewley's Café is Brambles restaurant. When the original shopping centre opened in Dundrum, just off the main street, in 1971, Bewleys was there as a café, but that too is long gone from what is now Dundrum Village Centre.

Blanchardstown Mills

This chain of Dublin- based shops had its heyday in the 1960s; it was way ahead of its time, because it sold all its grocery products loose. It had shops all over Dublin, from Dorset Street to Upper Baggot Street, beside Searson's pub.

Blanchardstown, old post office

O'Reilly's butchers shop in Blanchardstown in the early 1930s. Patrick O'Reilly, father of T.P. O'Reilly, is seen third from the left, While T.P. himself is seen as a small boy.
Mary Reynolds/Fingal county libraries

The old sub post office, with a shop at the front and the post office section at the back, was on the Main Street, but a St Vincent de Paul shop now stands on the site.

O' Reilly's butcher's shop was built on the site of the old police barracks on River Road. When T. P. O' Reilly was 16, in the 1940s, he had to take over the running of the shop when his father, Patrick, who had started the business suddenly died. Eventually, he relocated the shop to near Godley's draper's shop on the Main Street, opposite the Greyhound pub. The old butcher's shop now houses a florist's and a solicitor's office, while the old Garda barracks is now an adult education centre. The new Garda barracks was built at the end of Clonsilla Road in Blanchardstown in 1990.

Other old retail premises in Blanchardstown included Doyle's corner shop, in Church Avenue, which sold everything from fuel to groceries. Other tiny, family run shops operated from the front rooms of family homes, but all these small shops have now vanished.

Directly across the road from Doyle's corner shop was Ryan's garage, run for many years by Tim Ryan. Blanchardstown also once had two forges, both long gone. The larger one, Brien' s, was at the junction of the Main Street and Clonsilla Road. After it closed and was demolished, a galvanised tin shop was built on the site. The owner was known in the locality simply as Justin and he later opened a fruit and vegetable shop on the Main Street, opposite the Greyhound pub.

Booterstown

This south Co Dublin suburb once had a number of enticing shops that have now vanished.

McCabe's wine shop, at the corner of Cross Avenue and Mount Merrion Avenue, started in 1986 and for many years, had a treasure of wines that drew customers from far and near. But eventually, the creation of a bus lane in Mount Merrion Avenue by the local authority meant that customers could no longer park outside the shop. Many attempts to get planning permission to revamp the building also failed, so it was inevitable that the shop had to close. The building was sold in 2018 and the off licence has been transferred to the Gables restaurant and wine bar in Foxrock, run by the McCabe brothers, Jim and John.

Older shops in the area that have long since closed include Fitzells high class grocery store on Booterstown Avenue; there was also the Woodville Dairy run by a man called Woods, who was called 'Rubber Neck' by locals as he could swivel his long neck. He also had a talking parrot that used to sit on nearby telegraph wires squawking 'Buy your goods at Woods'. A second dairy on this road was the Primrose Dairy, whose advertising slogan was 'pure new milk, twice daily', from the owner's own herd of cows. Yet another long disappeared shop in Booterstown was Garvey's hardware shop, that used to display many of its lines, such as brushes and watering cans, outside, hanging from the front window, and on the pavement.

Boyers, North Earl Street

Boyer's department store closed down in January, 2016. At that stage, it was part of the Arnotts group, which had been taken over by Fitzwilliam Finance Partners. Operators had been sought to run Boyer' s, but none materialised, so the store was shut down, with the loss of 85 jobs, people who worked directly in the store as well as for concession holders.

Burton's the tailors

Burton's the tailors was at the junction of South Great George's Street and Dame Street for many years. The shop had opened in 1929. The premises is now a large Spar shop, but the words 'Tailors of Taste' can still be seen carved into the upper levels of the building.

Joe Byrne's bookies, Upper Leeson Street

The most famous sign in either part of Leeson Street is the one that proclaims "Joe Byrne bets here estd 1917". The traditional style bookie's shop is long gone, replaced by Green Design Build, but the sign remains intact on the front wall of the building that once housed the bookies. Not far away, at the junction of Upper Leeson Street and Sussex Road, what had once long been a bank branch, built in 1965, now houses a branch of Lisney's the estate agents.

Other shops to have disappeared from Upper Leeson Street including Dowling's grocery shop, whose origins dated back tio 1876 and which is now a Spar shop; Boland's tennis and sports shop; the sweet shop run by the two Brennan sisters for many years at 145 Upper Leeson Street and Maison Callan's ladies' hairdressers at number 138 on the same street.

Cabra Road shops

Among the old and vanished shops on the Cabra Road were Cullens, Downeys and Reads, selling many kinds of food. Reads specialised in groceries and it used to sell a lot of broken biscuits. But before they were sold, they were carefully weighed. Mr Read, who owned and ran the shop was known locally as "split the biscuit".

Camden Street

Camden Street has long been noted for its small shops, although like most other similar areas in Dublin, it's now become noted for its many restaurants, as well as Whelan's live music venue. One of the old style shops there was Gorevan's drapers' shop, an impressive building with four floors that had opened in 1927.

The old Irish Nationwide building society was founded in Upper Camden Street in 1873, changing its name nearly a century later to Irish Nationwide. After Gorevans closed down in the 1970s, the building society took over the premises as its headquarters, staying there for 20 years until its final move, to the old headquarters of the P. J. Carroll tobacco company on Grand Parade. The Irish Nationwide went spectacularly bust and in 2010, had to be bailed out by the State- and taxpayers- to the tune of €5. 4 billion.

Another noted place in Upper Camden Street, at the corner of Pleasants Street, was Cavey's car showrooms. Cavey's specialised in high value cars and at nearby Charlemont Place in the 1950s, had a small assembly plant where it put together, from kits, Jaguar XK 150 cars.

Two cinemas that existed long ago on Camden Street have found other uses. The old Camden Cinema at Upper Camden Street is now the headquarters of Concern Worldwide, the charity, while the Theatre de Luxe in Lower Camden Street is now an hotel and night club.

Capel Street

Des Kerins

For close on 200 years, Capel Street has managed to retain its idiosyncratic shops, giving the street perhaps the most unusual atmosphere of any retailing street in Dublin. However, many are concerned that currently planned developments in the immediate neighbourhood will dilute if not destroy Capel Street's unique charms. One shop that didn't survive was the Horse Shoe, at Number 85, which supplied what its name implied. In the 1960s, the shop was owned by a man called Kelly. A subsequent transformation saw it changed completely into En Grosse, a very modern grocery store, typical of the new style food retailers and restaurants on the street.

Carpenterstown, west Dublin

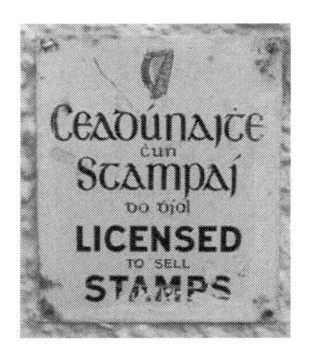

Mary Reynolds

Carpenterstown was long known for the Glen Stores, which opened in the early 1930s. Many local people worked in the shop over the years, which became a hub for the local community. Tony Reynolds remembers that not only did they have a telephone (Castleknock 86) and a radio, but that the post box and the number 80 bus stop were right outside.

The shop sold mostly groceries, but also bicycle lamps, mouse traps, kerosene and puncture repair kits. It even sold fireworks, until they were banned from sale in retail shops, following a fire in Furlong's shop in Donnybrook in 1947 (qv). Biscuits were stored in large tins and weighed out on request, while another once popular item, now very hard to find, was gur cake, a compacted square of Christmas pudding with a thin pastry crust on the top and bottom. Glass jars full of sweets were displayed behind the counter, with such delicacies as Peggy's Leg and Nancy Balls.

After much disputation with the postmistress in Castleknock village, the Reynolds got permission to sell postage stamps.

Another feature of the shop was the big brass cash register. But sadly, the shop has long since been demolished.

Peter Reynolds, the Glen Stores, Carpenterstown
Mary Reynolds

Castleknock

Mary Reynolds

In recent years, this one time village on the far side of the Phoenix Park has grown exponentially. But some of the old places remain, such as Myo' s, the leading pub in the area. Other pubs include Bradys and Kavanagh's. Myo' s, which goes back to best part of 200 years, was for long known as McKenna' s, but in the 1960s, it was bought by Myo O' Donnell, hence its name. It was substantially refurbished in 2017.

Mary Reynolds

But some older shops haven't been so lucky. For years, the Molloy family had a grocery shop and newagent combined in Castleknock, although by the 1970s, the Walsh family was running it. The shop later became Castleknock Flowers. It also had Horan's Hall to the rear, used for dances, plays and films. But after a long running planning dispute, the shop was demolished in 2018 to make way for a Lidl supermarket.

Mary Reynolds

Mary Reynolds

Mary Reynolds

Churchtown Stores

Dublin Gazette

The Churchtown Stores, on Braemor Road in Churchtown, was an amazing hardware shop that closed down at the start of 2018 after 25 years' trading. The store was run by brothers Barry, Fehan and Kieran, who opened it in February, 1988, after having had 25 years experience in the hardware business. The shop in Churchtown, which employed 20 people, was noted for having an exceptional range of products. If something a customer wanted wasn't in stock by any chance, it was quickly procured. The owners and the staff knew most of their customers by name. Retailing technology also bypassed the store; transactions were calculated on the back of an envelope, while the cash was kept in a rudimentary till.

Clery's, O' Connell Street

Clery's department store on O' Connell Street, opposite the GPO, dates back to 1853, when it was built to coincide with the great international exhibition in Dublin that year. The building was taken over by Michael Clery and a consortium of owners and it reopened, as Clery & Co., in 1884, after having stayed shut for a year. During the 1916 Easter Rising, the building was completely destroyed, but was rebuilt and opened once more in 1922. Clery's went bankrupt in 1940, then was taken over by the Guiney family. They ran it until 2004.

But through the years, Clery's remained the go- to place in the city centre for fashions and household goods, with concessionaires being an important part of its retail mix. It went into receivership in 2012 and was eventually taken over by the Natrium consortium, which closed down the store in 2015, putting everyone working in Clery's out of a job. Then in October, 2018, yet another takeover was announced and the new consortium said that it expected to begin construction work on a complete renovation of the building.

One important part of Clery's will remain, the clock on its front façade. Underneath the Clery's clock has been a meeting place for many generations of Dubliners.

Clontarf Road

For many years, this main road on Dublin's northside had a plethora of shops, but all have long since vanished, changed into a variety of new style outlets.

At the end of the 1960s, B. M. Fitzpatrick ran a shop at Number 12 that sold antique furniture, but it was later turned over to a completely different use, the Dom Bosco home for homeless boys. Number 47A once housed O' Neill's provisions' shop, but it later became an outlet for ladies' handbags. Andrew Hennessy's chemist's shop, together with Horgan's the hairdressers, became transformed into a beauty salon and a shop that sold conservatories. J. J. Heagney's sweet shop at Number 49 (these days, sweet shops are a very endangered species) was turned into a travel agent's shop, while John Keys, the tobacconist at Number 50 turned into a Tandoori restaurant and a ladies' wear shop.

What was, in the 1960s, Gidding's supermarket at Number 52 did a complete transformation into a dry cleaners, while Gillen's food market at Number 54 didn't go through such a profound change, becoming La Costa takeaway foods. The long vanished Mervue Confections, once renowned for its cakes, was at Number 192. It made the most startling transformation of all, into the Oriental Healing house, while auctioneers, chemists and a beauty salon also occupied the former cake shop. At Number 197B, Clontarf Road had another bakery and confectionery shop, O' Donnell' s, which progressed to being occupied by a turf accountant and the Muscle Shop. The old style of shops on the Clontarf Road five decades ago has undergone a mighty transformation in the intervening years.

Combridge's shop, Grafton Street

For many years, Combridge's fine art shop was a prominent feature of Grafton Street, situated close to where Marks & Spencer is now located. Combridge's had been founded in 1907 and after it left Grafton Street, it eventually relocated to its present address in South William Street. A large sign for Combridge's can still be seen on an exterior wall of The Bailey pub on Duke Street.

Dandelion Market

In many ways, this was the first "hippy" market in Dublin and was enormously popular as it reflected a very contemporary laid back lifestyle. The market had started in 1970 in Pembroke Lane, just off Lower Pembroke Street, then it moved the following year, 1971, to Leeson Close, off Lower Leeson Street. But in 1973, it moved to a disused warehouse in South King Street, where it lasted for 11 years. It was said that you could buy anything these from paintings to knitwear, vintage clothes, footwear, household furnishings and record players. It was one of the places where a newly formed band called U2 performed one of their first gigs. The Dandelion Market closed down in 1981 and the site was eventually subsumed into the St Stephen's Green shopping centre.

Dawson Street

At the top of Dawson Street, a couple of legendary shops have long since gone. Harry Moore started his shop in 1943 and for many years, he was the person to go to for radio sets, later expanded in TV sets and other audio- visual equipment. Almost next to his shop was Alys Glennon's fashion shop, at the corner of Dawson Street and St Stephen's Green.

Further down that side of Dawson Street, right beside St Ann's Church of Ireland, Bective Electrical was a familiar firm for many years. Dooly's antiques shop was also once a familiar sight on the street.

On the opposite side of Dawson Street, Needlecraft was started in 1938 by Jack and Julieann Flavin; eventually, it was taken over by Noel, son of Jack, and his wife, Breed, who ran the shop until they retired and closed it in 2001. It had been one of the last surviving family owned and run shops in the city centre. With its two bay windows, full of hand- knitted items, hand written signs and old fashioned interior, it was the place to go for anything to do with knitting and needlecraft. Today, the premises are occupied by the Celtic whiskey shop and Wines on the Green. A newer shop, almost beside Needlecraft, has also faded from view, the Austrian-run Auric patisserie, which brought a new style of pastry making and selling to the city centre.

Deegan's newsagents, South Anne Street

For over 50 years, Deegan's small newsagents at 19, South Anne Street was a popular place for newspapers and magazines. The shop was small, with two display windows, one large, the other small, on either side of the front door. It closed down over five years ago and the premises have been completely transformed, as has much of the rest of the street. What was Deegan's is now Deirdre O' Connell's high class jewellery outlet.

Dockrell's, South Great George's Street

Dockrell's was a noted hardware store that traded in South Great George's Street for the best part of a century, until it closed down in the 1980s. The store had been built in 1888. Then part of it became a shoe retailer, but from the early 1990s, the former store was left derelict, apart from an Indian restaurant that survived until 2015. Now there are plans to develop a 100 bedroom hotel on the site, but the original brick façade will be retained.

Dolphin Discs

Dolphin Discs was once a very popular record shop; its main outlet was in Talbot Street, while in nearby Marlborough Street, it had two shops facing each other. The shops lasted for 40 years; Dolphin Discs closed its doors for the last time in 2012.

Donnybrook's old shops

Donnybrook in south Dublin is a classic example of a local village that has changed beyond all belief in the past few years, as all its old shops have disappeared.

Perhaps its best- known shop was Furlong's newsagents, close to the junction of Morehampton Road and Marlborough Road. It had traded for the best part of 80 years and survived a great tragedy in the late 1940s. The stock of fireworks being kept at the back of the shop for Halloween caught fire and a shop assistant was killed in the blaze. Fortunately, a young Gerry Callanan, whose parents then ran the shop, managed to escape unharmed and for many more years, he ran the shop until he retired a decade ago.

Furlong's was an unofficial social club for Donnybrook and the great and the good, as well as the not so good, congregated there to exchange the latest local news and scandals, encouraged by Gerry, who always had a mischievous side to his character. After he retired, to devote more time to the Fitzwilliam Lawn Tennis Club, the shop lay derelict for a number of years until it was taken over by Boots. It's now a very efficient but totally characterless pharmacy, while that part of Morehampton Road still has the smaller but family run Brady's Morehampton Pharmacy.

Almost next door to Furlong's for many years was Nyland' s, an old fashioned traditional grocery shop, but it too closed down, as did the adjacent O' Connor's hardware store, which always had a fine stock of household items. Yet another vanished shop from this part of Donnybrook was Quinlan's bakery shop, noted for its exquisite cakes. Eileen's ladies hairdressers was a popular place for many years, long since replaced by Di Milo, which is now at the other end of Donnybrook, near the fire station. Garages too have disappeared or changed completely. The old Donnybrook Fair supermarket became the starting place for the group of the same name, taken over in 2018 by Musgraves in Cork, the people behind Super Valu and Centra. For many years, the Morehampton petrol station stood almost next to Furlong's complete with petrol pump on the footpath. A similar arrangement was in place for the old garage that was in place next door to Madigan's pub, now O' Connell's restaurant.

At the other end of Donnybrook, near the Garda station, another old fashioned grocery shop also closed down, Stynes, which was replaced by the Balti restaurant. Just across the road from Stynes was Woods' Spar supermarket, which had been run in the 1960s by the Hickeys. Woods' supermarket has now been replaced by a 24 hour Spar supermarket. At this end of Donnybrook, too, another long established retailer, Molloy' s, which traded in fish and other delicacies, and Cunningham's radio shop, have now been replaced by more modern retail outlets. The most recent closure in Donnybrook was of the Bank of Ireland branch, in 2018, which has now been replaced by a home furnishing shop. The old branch of the First National Building Society eventually became a branch of the Ulster Bank, but that has long since been boarded up.

Two other shops in Donnybrook that have long since ceased to exist show how much retailing patterns have changed. The two travel shops that once traded in Donnybrook have also long ceased to exist, Panorama Travel and Donnybrook Travel. These days, most travel bookings are done online, thereby wiping out most travel shops.

Another shop in Donnybrook that has long since vanished into oblivion- the fire station is now on the site, was Hodges Figgis bookshop. But fortunately, the main Hodges Figgis bookshop in Dawson Street is still going strong.

The most recent and dramatic shop closure in Donnybrook was Fox' s, which for seven decades was a very popular spot for people buying fruit and vegetables. It closed down two years ago, but it's future use still hasn't been revealed.

Even the pubs in Donnybrook have felt the winds of change. Kielys closed down in 2018; it once had an art gallery on its first floor, giving rise to the expression that it was one of the few places in Dublin where art was above drink. Madigans has been turned into a restaurant and McCloskey's pub is set to be redeveloped into an apartment complex. Donnybrook now has one remaining pub, the old Long's pub, which was sold in November, 2012. It was subsequently converted into Arthur Maynes' pub, which has interesting windows full of old bottles.

Dunn's fish shop and deli, Upper Baggot Street

Dunn' s, the Dublin fish company which is still trading, had a retail outlet at Upper Baggot Street until 25 years ago. The shop was a very elegant outlet for fresh fish and a great variety of deli items, but after it closed down, it was transformed into an altogether more prosaic outlet, a Burger King restaurant.

Dunwell's shoe repairs, Phibsboro'

Harry Havelin

Dunwell's shoe repair shop stood at the corner of Goldsmith Street and the North Circular Road. The firm had a number of shoe repair shops around the city, long since gone. The most prominent name in shoe repairs in Dublin these days is C & D Shoes.

ESB shop, Fleet Street

record breaking crowds at the old ESB shop in Fleet Street, Dublin, on Easter Tuesday, 1961.
ESB Archives

For many years, the spacious ESB shop in Fleet Street was where many people and families went to pay their electricity bills. This shop was opened in 1946. It experienced its busiest day ever on April 4, 1961, when huge crowds poured in to pay their bills. The combination of children's allowances being paid that day and an imminent gas strike prompted the crowds and the sales of kettles were especially dramatic. The showrooms closed down in 2005; these days, most people pay their electricity bills online or by direct debit, so the idea of going to an ESB showroom to pay the bill has become totally old fashioned.

Findlater's

Findlater's was an old chain of grocery shops that once flourished throughout the greater Dublin area. The Findlater family has its roots in Scotland and Alexander Findlater (1823-1873) founded the shops in Dublin in the 1820s. They sold both groceries and alcoholic drinks. The shops stretched from Howth to Greystones, taking in such places as Upper Baggot Street (now a branch of Tesco), Dundrum, Foxrock and Rathmines. Findlaters, which had its headquarters at Upper O' Connell Street, converted its shop at Wicklow Street, just off Grafton Street, into a supermarket in the late 1960s, but neither it nor a branch in the then new Stillorgan shopping centre survived. Findlater's had missed the great supermarket revolution that swept Ireland in the 1960s.

But one of the Findlaters, Alex, opened a wine shop at Upper Rathmines Road in 1974 and went on to set up a wine merchant's business in part of the old railway station at the top of Harcourt Street. It was bought by the C & C group in 2001.

John J. Finlay, Lower Camden Street

This well- known hardware store traded in Lower Camden Street for well over 50 years.

First National Building Society

This had been founded in 1861, in what is now Pearse Street, as the Workingman's Benefit Building Society. It changed its name to the First National Building Society in 1960. After taking over a number of smaller building societies, such as the one run by Guinness for its workers, it changed its status to become a publicly quoted company in 1998, when it also changed its name to First Active. In 2004, it was acquired by the Royal Bank of Scotland, which owns Ulster Bank. First Active was merged with the Ulster Bank in late 2009 and within three months, was closed down.

The First National Building Society had a branch network covering the whole of Ireland; in Dublin, it had branches in such places as Artane, Donnybrook, Drumcondra, Dundrum, Phibsboro and the corner of Grafton Street and Suffolk Street.

Five Star supermarkets

Five Star supermarkets were one of the first supermarket groups to start up in the 1960s, when the supermarket revolution in Ireland really got going. H. Williams, a long established chain of grocery shops, started the first supermarket in Ireland at Henry Street, Dublin, in 1959. Ironically, when sales tax was introduced by a Fianna Fáil government and came into operation in 1963, it proved a death knell for many smaller family run grocery shops and facilitated the spread of supermarkets.

As for H. Williams, It collapsed in 1987 after a supermarket price war. Five Star supermarkets, which had been owned by D. E. Williams, the then owners of Tullamore Dew whiskey and a similarly named liqueur brand, also faded out of the market completely. Its head office was in Gresham House, Marine Road, Dún Laoghaire, which now houses the headquarters of Tesco Ireland. Tesco made its second attempt at the Irish grocery market in 1997 when it took over Quinnsworth supermarkets, which it soon rebranded as Tesco.

Foster Stores, Mount Merrion Avenue

The Foster Stores, at the top of Mount Merrion Avenue, in south Co Dublin, were started in 1934 by the Collins Sisters. They converted the old stables, part of the farm at Owenstown House, into a shop, which traded in groceries and newspapers for many years.

German pork butchers

Dublin was once renowned for the number of German pork butchers it had. The Haffners had shops in South Great George's Street and Henry Street, while the Olhausens had shops in Camden Street and Talbot Street. The Retz family also had a pork butcher's shop in Camden Street. The Speidel brothers had shops in Talbot Street as well as on the North Strand Road, the Phibsoboro' Road and Marino Mart. Charles Seezer had a shop at 40, Thomas Street, whilst on the southside, Herman Horlacher had shops in both upper and lower George's Street in Dún Laoghaire and another member of the same family, August Horlacher, had a shop at 2c Main Street, Blackrock.

In Sandymount, Karl Strecker founded a butcher's shop on Sandymount Road in Sandymount village when he arrived from Germany in 1927. Around 30 years later, he came to an unfortunate end when he fell off his horse while out riding on Bray

Head. But despite the demise of all these shops, in recent years, the Haffner and Olhausen brand names have lived on.

Glasnevin

Pauline Brennan

The Ark on Botanic Road in Glasnevin, between the canal and Lindsay Road, was a popular shop many years ago selling groceries and confectionery. Eithne McKeon recalls that money was very scarce during the Emergency of the second world war but that on the odd morning when going to school at Holy Faith in Iona Road, her mother gave Eithne and her sister a penny for an ice cream wafer. They used to go into the Ark and Eithne, as the older sister, would ask for a penny wafer, cut in two. On one particular occasion, the two girls behind the counter began to laugh at this request, so Eithne and her sister left the Ark, highly embarrassed and never darkened its doors again.

They transferred their custom to Payantake on the same stretch of Botanic Road, where they could get two sticks of spaghetti for a penny.

Also in Glasnevin, on Prospect Avenue, was Scullys. Kathleen and Joe Scully bought the shop in 1949; it had been Carrolls.

Scullys opened all day, from Mondays to Saturdays, and for a half day on Sunday. The shop was basically a grocery shop, but it sold everything from a spool of thread, balls of blue starch and Mrs Cullen's Powders, to rashers, Kearns sausages, milk, loose buttermilk from a creamery can to turkeys at Christmas. Dry goods like sugar had to be weighed up and bagged. Biscuits were sold loose from rows of tins in front of the counter, either by the half pound or the pound. The counter itself was quite small, six feet by three ft.

Kathleen Scully had a faithful assistant for many years, Colette Gorman. There were several other small shops in the neighbourhood, an area close to Glasnevin cemetery, such as Brennans, the Cottage Stores, the Dublin House and Hands.

Pauline Brennan, nee Scully, remembers that she and her four brothers, all had to take turns in helping out in the shop, and they had to be smart and businesslike. On one occasion when a customer came in, she and one of her brothers were disputing whose turn it was to serve, until they were brought down to earth with a sharp telling off from the customer.

Saturday was always a very busy day, when the orders had to be made up and delivered. Customers generally had the same order every week, such as a pound of butter, a quarter pound of tea, a pound of rashers (gammon, back or streaky), sausages, and perhaps a quarter pound of loose biscuits. The Scully children liked to go with their father when he was delivering orders; occasionally, there was sixpence from a grateful custo, ers.

Many of the Scully's customers operated on the "book" system, under which items bought were paid for at a later date. Pauline remembers her mother making up these accounts at night time and marvelled at her speed in totting up pounds, shillings and pence. The shop was also a very sociable place and Kathleen Scully helped many customers through their trials and tribulations and they were assured that everything they said to her was treated with the utmost confidentiality.

Sadly, the arrival of supermarkets in Phibsboro' started the decline of the small shops in the area. The Scullys used to find it very annoying to answer a knock on the door late at night, by someone who was looking for a bottle of milk or a packet of cigarettes. That same person would have passed the front of the Scullys' shop earlier on with a bag of groceries from the supermarket. Scully's shop eventually closed in 1990.

Grafton Street arcades

Grafton Street once had two arcades, Grafton Arcade, near the present day McDonald' s, and Creation Arcade, on the far side of the junction with Duke Street. The Grafton Arcade was redeveloped in 2010 while subsequently, Creation Arcade, named after the magazine publishers that were once based there, was also redeveloped out of existence.

Greene's bookshop, Clare Street

This famed Dublin bookshop closed down in May, 2007, when it switched to online trading from a warehouse on the Sandyford industrial estate in south Co Dublin. Greene's was founded in 1843 and in 1912, it was taken over by Herbert H. Pembrey. Herbert, his son, and the younger Herbert's son, Eric, eventually took over the running of the bookshop. Eventually, in 1958, the lending library side of the business was closed.

Both Herbert the son and Herbert' son Eric, died the same year, 2000. In its last years in the 250 year old building in Clare Street that also doubled as a sub post office, Greene's was run by David Pembrey. The bookshop was famed for its glass canopy and beneath that canopy were trays full of old books, supported on trestles.

General Sales Shop, Portobello

One of the traditional shops in the Portobello district was the General Sales Shop, on Clanbrassil Street. It lived up to its reputation by selling a wide range of goods, everything from second hand books to ornaments and decorative items for the home.

Grocer Jack, 1967 song

This song, which became an unexpected chart hit across Europe, featured an old- fashioned grocer who sold his wares to inhabitants of his village, going from door- to- door. He was much mocked by local children, but after he died, people who had taken his service for granted mourned him and the loss of the service he provided, while for children, he became a much loved figure in retrospect. The song captured perfectly the way in which so many small, family owned shops were swept away in the 1960s by the new style supermarkets.

Fred Hanna' s, Nassau Street

Hanna's bookshop in Nassau Street dated back to the 1840s; the Hanna family took over in 1907 and ran it until 1999, when the business was sold to Eason' s. The bookshop had for many years supplied books to students at Trinity College, on the other side of Nassau Street. The last member of the Hanna family to run the business was Fred Hanna, who died in 2011, aged 77; he had been in charge for 47 years. After the sale, the building adjacent to Hanna's was redeveloped and the brand new shop that opened at basement level has been an Eason's outlet, selling books and many stationery and gift items, right up to the present day.

Harold's Cross old shops

The oldest shop in Harold's Cross is Delaney's bicycle shop at 7, Harold's Cross Road, just past the canal bridge. Thomas Delaney came from Co Kildare to start the shop in 1917 and it still continues today, run his great grandsons, Brian and Paul. Other nearby shops included Mrs Daly' s, a sister of Cearbhaill Ó Dalaigh, a former President. Then a relative, Sineád Ó Cadhla, took it over and ran it for many years, until 1971.She died in 1993. In later years, it became known as The Gem, selling sweets and light groceries. For a while, there was also a piano shop on this terrace, then the Cuala Dairy shop and then two hairdressers. Today, Miss World Hair and the Bridge Babes can be found on the site.

Hector Grey, Liffey Street

Hector Grey was one of the best- known retailers in Dublin from the 1950s until the 1970s. He was a Scot who came to Dublin to make his fortune, which he did, selling vast quantitites of bric à brac at knockdown prices. Hector Grey wasn't his real name; he had been christened Hector Scott.

He was renowned for his sales spiels, in which he told endless stories to whip up public interest. He had a pitch on the north quays, near the Ha' Penny Bridge and these attracted great crowds in search of a good yarn and even more importantly, a good bargain. Hector Grey also had a shop in Liffey Street for many years, opposite what is now the side entrance to Marks & Spencer's store in Mary Street. He died in Dublin in 1985, aged 83.

Hendricks Gallery

For many years, this was the perfect shop window at 119 St Stephen's Green, near the College of Surgeons, for many Irish artists. There they could display and sell their works of art. It was opened by Ritchie Hendricks in 1956, then from the 1969 until 1983, it became the David Hendricks Gallery. Finally, in 1984, that was shortened to the Hendricks Gallery, which lasted for a mere five years, until 1989.

HMV Records, Grafton Street

HMV Records opened in the old Woolworth's store at the top of Grafton Street; the record shop opened in 1986, after the demise of Woolworth's in Ireland. For many years, it was a very popular record store. The other half of the old building was occupied by Next, a fashion retailer. But in 2013, HMV Ireland went into liquidation and all its stores in Ireland closed. It was bought by a firm called Hilco Capital Ireland, but this and all its other stores in Ireland closed in 2016, when the firm opted for online trading.

Hough's shop, Crumlin Road

Hough's general grocery shop traded for many years from the 1940s, run by Michael Hough. It sold a wide variety of grocery items, while it also did a big trade in newspapers. Hough's even sold fish and meat, in fact everything a household could need. The shop even had a great variety of sweets in tall glass jars. The shop lasted for 40 years, before closing. One of the children of Michael Hough and his wife Patricia was a well- known RTÉ presenter, now retired, Kevin Hough.

Imco, Merrion Road

The Imco dry cleaning firm had its head office on the Merrion Road, opposite the present day Tara Towers Hotel, itself due to be redeveloped shortly. The Imco building had a striking Art Deco style tower, which was a local landmark. Imco closed down in

1974, the building on the Merrion Road, including the tower, were demolished to make way for a mundane office block.

Irish Times shops, Westmoreland Street and D' Olier Street

For many years, The Irish Times had shops, first on Westmoreland Street, then on D' Olier Street, before the newspaper moved, a decade ago, to new premises in Tara Street. The Westmoreland Street shop was very old fashioned, with little room for counters, but in time, this side of Westmoreland Street, including the old EBS building society premises at the corner of Fleet Street, was extensively redeveloped. When The Irish Times closed down its shop in Westmoreland Street, it opened a more modern shop in D' Olier Street. But since the newspaper moved to Tara Street, its old site, which ran from D' Olier Street to Westmoreland Street and which was bounded on one side by Fleet Street, has been completely redeveloped.

Irish Yeast Company, College Street

Lisa Cassidy/Built Dublin

For many years, the Irish Yeast Company shop, its windows full of cats, was one of the oldest shops in Dublin. The building it was in dates back to 1750, but the yeast firm dated back to 1890, when it was started to sell yeast to bakeries all over Ireland. For many years, it was managed by John Moreland. But with the arrival of supermarkets in the 1960s, their sales of cheaper, mass produced bread ate into the sales of the yeast company. In more recent years, home baking became much more technically sophisticated and the traditional yeast made by the company was replaced by dried yeast. But the shop continued to sell all kinds of equipment connected with baking.

After the death of John Moreland, the shop and the rest of the building at College Green was put up for sale. However, development opportunities for the building are limited, as it's a listed structure. The new owners wanted to merge the old Yeast Company shop with Bowe's pub in Fleet Street, but this plan was rejected by Dublin City Council in February, 2019.

Iveagh Stores, New Bride Street

Michael Doyle

The Iveagh Stores began trading in 1903 as a greengrocers; in subsequent years, other traders took over the premises, so that in became, in turn, a dairy, a takeaway and a branch of the Trustee Savings Bank. By 2019, it had become an eye clinic, under the direction of the Technological University of Dublin. This photograph was taken in 1971 by Michael Doyle.

Johnston, Mooney & O' Brien bakery shop, Ballsbridge

The renowned Dublin bakery firm was formed in 1889 from the amalgamation of three smaller bakeries and moved into a brand new bakery on the banks of the River Dodder, close to the bridge in Ballsbridge. It closed its Ballsbridge bakery exactly a century later, in 1989, moving to a site in Finglas, while it also started a bun bakery in Co Meath. The firm continues to trade successfully.

While the bakery at Ballsbridge was a huge enterprise, still employing nearly 500 people by the time it closed, it also had a shop that faced Ballsbridge Terrace. For many years, people going to the nearby Herbert Park bought bread and cakes there for picnics. After the bakery was closed, it was demolished and the Herbert Park Hotel and Embassy House were built on the site.

Kennedy & McSharry

This long established gents' outfitters, founded in 1890, long had an extensive shop on Nassau Street, but that closed down in 2012. The firm then moved to the Powerscourt Town House Centre.

Keogh's bookshop, Phibsboro'

Harry Havelin

Keogh's bookshop was a feature of Berkeley Road, Phibsboro' for many years, directly opposite the Mater Hospital. Its windows, either side of the entrance, were always crammed with great displays of books, but like many other bookshops, it is long since past history.

Laundries

Laundries were long a part of the retail scene in Dublin. The Dartry Laundry in 1900 was claimed to be the second largest in these islands; the firm also had an offshoot, the Dartry Dye Works and the two companies merged in 1955 as the Dublin Laundry and the Dartry Dye Works. It also had a number of branches throughout the city. Other laundries included the Kelso and the Swastika, but by the mid- 1980s, the era of the laundries was fast coming to an end, as many households were starting to install washing machines.

The Swastika Laundry had been started in 1912 by John W. Brittain, who had already founded two other laundries in Dublin, the Metropolitan Laundry and the White Heather. The name of the Swastika Laundry came from a sign used in India as a symbol of divinity and spirituality, long before it was appropriated for the Nazi party in Germany. In 1956, the Swastika employed Richard Kingston, later to become a well- known artist, as their resident designer. He set up a studio for the laundry, which produced everything from packaging and posters to shop interiors, and he effected a complete change of image for the laundry. He stayed in that full- time job until 1964, but remained on after that, for a few more years, as a consultant.

But in 1987, the Spring Grove laundry bought the Swastika and its three affiliated companies, Monarch Laundry, Dunlop Laundry and Bells Dry Cleaners. The Englishman who was running the Spring Grove immediately decided to get rid of the Swastika image. The old laundry headquarters, on Shelbourne Road, Ballsbridge, was redeveped nearly 20 years, but the old chimney from the laundry was retained.

Liptons

Liptons is a long vanished name in Dublin retailing, noted in the 1960s for its chain of grocery shops, one in Grafton Street, others in the suburbs. But such was the pace of supermarket innovation in the 1960s that older shops, like Liptons, disappeared within a decade and are often little remembered today.

Little Jerusalem

Many Jewish people came to Ireland, fleeing persecution in eastern Europe, in the 1870s and they settled in the Clanbrassil Street area. It and all its Jewish shops became known as Little Jerusalem, although all those old shops are long gone. The new migrants became fully absorbed into the professional, trades and manufacturing walks of life and as they became more prosperous, they moved to such areas as the South Circular Road, Longwood Avenue, Bloomfield Avenue and other parts of Portobello, before migrating to even better off areas, such as Terenure.

Such was the involvement of Jewish workers in the garment industry in this part of south Dublin that in 1908, Jewish textile workers started the International Tailors, Machinists and Pressers' trade union, remembered by a plaque next door to the Concern Worldwide headquarters on Upper Camden Street.

Although the old Jewish shops have long since disappeared, one, the Bretzel Bakery in Lennox Street, is still going strong; it started off as a Kosher bakery. The Jewish Museum in Portobello has much detail on the old Jewish shops in this part of Dublin.

Lucan

Among the venerable old shops in Lucan was the Coffee House, a long time favourite meeting place for people living in the area. It was demolished in 1984. Joe Collins & Son butchers has traded in Lucan for a century and most recently has been run by Niall Collins. The shop was put up for sale in 2018.

Another shop in Lucan also seems very archaic now, although it was comparatively recent. In 1983, a new computer shop opened in the village and it advertised jobs for people with skills in handling Commodore, Oric and Sinclair computers, brands that are now long forgotten.

Madam Nora's, Lower O'Connell Street

Madam Nora's was an elegant shop for ladies' fashions in Lower O' Connell Street. According to Bridie Armstrong, it always had a great window display, while the stock inside included lovely handbags, umbrellas and gloves. Collette Modes in South Great George's Street was another great ladies' fashion shop, while the Silk Mills' shop in Dorset Street was equally renowned.

Magill's deli, Clarendon Street

Magill's delicatessen shop at number 14, Clarendon Street, ran for over five decades, selling many Italian sourced foods, including meats and cheeses. The interior of the shop was dark and cramped, but was very like the type of vintage charcuterie found in Italy, with tantalising smells to match. Magill's was taken over in 1999 by Kim Condon, who closed her food shop in Rathgar to take over the running of Magills. Sadly, today, the shop is all shuttered up, its food delicacies a thing of the past.

But next door, on the corner of Clarendon Street and Johnson's Court, just opposite the back of the Powerscourt Town House Centre, Johnson Court Antiques is still thriving.

Maison Prost hairdressers, St Stephen's Green

Maison Prost was a noted ladies' hairdressers at 24 St Stephen's Green North. It thrived in the early part of the 20th century, renowned not only for its hair styling, but also for its electrolysis, hair tinting, chiropody and manicures; it even had its own brand of perfume. The salon managed to keep going until the 1960s, when the site was redeveloped and became something rather more mundane, the headquarters of an estate agents.

Mapother's, Sandymount Green

Sandymount by Hugh Oram

For many years, Mapother's newsagents on Sandymount Green, run by Harry Mapother and his wife Lilly, was a popular retail outlet for newspapers, magazines and sweets. They retired in early 1999 and the shop closed down. Soon afterwards, the shop and the upstairs living accommodation was sold and the building was turned into an art gallery as well as auction rooms for a local estate agent.

Marlborough Street

One of the long- time fixtures on Marlborough Street, which runs parallel to O' Connell Street, was the CIE Club at Number 98, where bus workers at CIE, the State owned transport company, could relax in the company of comrades. But it has long gone, along with similar working people's clubs, such as the City of Dublin Working Mens' club at 10 Wellington Quay.

Mason's opticians

This firm is one of the longest established in Dublin, dating back over 200 years. For much of the 20th century, it was located in Dame Street in the city centre, where it operated until the 1970s. It's now known as Mason Technology, based on the South Circular Road. Alongside Mason's when it was in Dame Street were other retailing legends, such as Hely' s, the stationers and printers; Callaghan' s, famed for its riding gear and Siberry' s, men's outfitters.

Max photographic studios

For many years, this was the leading photographic studio in the city centre, along with other such well- known studios as Lafayette. The Max studios opened at 55 Lower O' Connell Street in 1953 and traded as such until 1979. There was a five year hiatus before it reopened in 1984 as Renard Cameo Studios. But that new lease of life was shortlived; the studios finally closed down two years later, in 1986.

May's music shop, St Stephen's Green

This small music shop sold mainly sheet music and traded for well over 50 years on St Stephen's Green, owned by the May family, who lived in Donnybrook. Frederick May (1911- 1985) was the musical scion of the family, who studied in London and Vienna before returning to Dublin in 1936. He then became the musical director of the Abbey Theatre for 15 years. He also composed a limited number of works, which had a very European sound, while he also arranged music. He had a serious lifelong hearing disability, which affected his career. The family run music shop eventually closed down and was demolished to make way for the St Stephen's Green shopping centre.

McBirney' s, Aston Quay

McBirney's old department store on Aston Quay always advertised itself as "40 paces from O' Connell Bridge". The store had been built in the early 20th century and lasted for most of that century, closing down in 1984. After it shut, the building was bought by Richard Branson, who turned it into a Virgin Megastore, which lasted for two decades. It was sold on again in the early years of this century and the ground floor was turned into a Super Valu supermarket.

Milky Way, Harcourt Street

Joan Purcell

Throughout the 1960s and the 1970s, the Milky Way was a favourite stopping off point for people going home from the ballroom at the top of Harcourt Street. Joan Purcell, who now lives in Thurles, Co Tipperary, remembers vividly that walking home with a friend form the Civil Cems (the civil and chemical engineering students) regular hop in the Four Provinces ballroom, they stopped off at the Milky Way to buy a half bottle of milk, with tinfoil top (now long gone) and a Lapwing, whose equivalent today is a Penguin bar. Joan says that their journey home to Terenure Road East meant walking, as taxis were too expensive. On the way home, she met the man who she married five years later; they have now been married 50 years.

Mitchell's, Kildare Street

The Mitchell's wine firm grew out of the Mitchell's café in Grafton Street (the premises were turned into the first McDonalds in Ireland over 30 years ago) and the Mitchell's wine shop opened at 21 Kildare Street in 1887. For many years, the firm bottled its own rum, port and sherry, and other drinks, in the basement. In 1978, Mitchell's converted its basement cellars into a restaurant and wine bar, which lasted until 1999. Then Bruno's restaurant took over, but it too has come and gone. In 2008, Mitchell's sold its premises in Kildare Street and moved its headquarters to the CHQ building, beside the IFSC. But today, Mitchell's remains the only wine retailer of its vintage still owned and run by descendents of the founders.

Near to the old Mitchell's shop in Kildare Street was Kildare Antiques at Number 19, one of several Dublin city centre antique shops, including some along the quays, which have succumbed to changes in retail patterns.

Monument Creameries

The Monument Creameries once had a chain of shops all over Dublin, renowned for selling bakery and fresh food products, such as butter, in the days before refrigeration had come into universal retail use. A once familiar sight in all its shops was one pound shapes of butter being paddled into shape from huge blocks of butter that rested on the counter. Despite the lack of refrigeration, none of the products ever went off.

The firm had been started in 1919 in Parnell Street and took its name from the nearby Parnell Monument. It was run by Séamus Ryan and his wife Agnes Ryan. Séamus died young, in 1933, but he was such a well-known political figure that he was given a State funeral. Agnes carried on the business, which went into liquidation and closed in 1966, shortly after her death. The 33 strong chain of shops, everywhere from Dawson Street to Upper Baggot Street and Stillorgan had gone into a steep decline with the advent of supermarkets in the early 1960s.

North King Street

Harry Havelin

Two of the old shops there that have long since vanished were Muldoons, at Number 101, which sold fish and poultry in the

1960s and Patterson's saddlers and O' Sullivan Bros radio and electrical shop at Number 73. But Muldoon's old shop continued in the ownership of Albert Muldoon for many years afterwards.

Harry Havelin

Oddbins off licences

Oddbins, a UK- based chain of off licences, came to Ireland in the late 1990s and opened four shops in the Dublin area, at Upper Baggot Street, Churchtown, Blackrock and on the Clontarf Road. They all closed down in 2011 with the demise of the chain.

The shop in Upper Baggot Street reopened as Baggot Street Wines, in July, 2011, and has since built up a formidable reputation for its selection of wines and spirits. Its adjacent Cave restaurant was undergoing refurbishment at the time of writing. The

Blackrock shop became El Cellar, a Spanish style tapas bar and also an off licence, while the Oddbins shop at 360 Clontarf Road was turned into 360 Cycles. Before Oddbins came along, the shop had belonged to Patrick Bennett, a spirit grocer, in the old tradition of grocery retailing in Ireland, when part of the premises would be given over to selling alcoholic drinks.

O'Dwyers, Beggar's Bush

O'Dwyer family

O' Dwyer's was an old fashioned grocery shop at the foot of Haddington Road, at Beggar's Bush. The small shop had a great selection of grocery items, as well as sweets and cigarettes. It was a prominent shop in the area in the earlier years of the 20th century, but it and the block it was in, which also included Ryan's pub, were eventually demolished to make way for the modern Ryan's pub, itself substantially remodelled in recent years. The little laneway at the side of O' Dwyer' s, Lansdowne Park, used to have a terrace of modest two storey houses in the old days, but it has been totally redeveloped during the past three decades.

Old County Road, Crumlin

The right hand side of Old County Road once had a veritable bazaar of shops in the 1960s, all of which have now closed down, with many varieties of new outlets taking their place.

Christine, the hair stylist at Number 93, has long since vanished, as has James McGonigle, the grocer at Number 97, and Denis Quinlan, the draper at Number 99. Hugh Kavanagh's grocery shop at Number 105 eventually metamorphosed into Kay's grocery shop, while Furlong's pork butcher's shop at Number 105A, turned into the Vanilla Room beauty salon.

At least, Cluskey's pork butchers at Number 113 was transformed into something similar, County Meats, run by a man called Sheary. Michael Sinnott's grocery shop at Number 117 changed into Kelly's mini market, while Tony's sweet shop at Number 123A, run by Anthony Verracchia, changed into a ladies' hairdressing salon and an Indian restaurant. In the 1960s, the last shop on that side of the Old County Road, was Frank Colgan's fruit and vegetable shop, but later, the site became vacant.

Old Curiosity Shop, Merchant's Arch

This old shop certainly lived up to its name, having a great variety of second- hand goods in its windows and its interior, a real treasure trove of antique 'goodies'.

Old fishing tackle shops

Shops selling fishing tackle can often come and go and two of those who disappeared were the Bestak shop at 24 Essex Quay, which was successful in the 1960s and from the same time frame, the Moorkens shop at 13 Main Street in Blackrock.

Peat's, Parnell Street

In the 1970s and early 1980s, as many of Dublin's traditional shops were being swept away in the retail revolution, Pat Murray, a resident of Ballbridge and someone with a keen interest in local history, photographed many of these shops before they passed from existence and memory. He took about 150 photographs and eventually, donated the whole collection to the Irish Architectural Archive in Merrion Square, where they can be seen today.

Pim's department store, South Great George's Street

Pim's was once a vast department store, owned by a Quaker family, who diversified from poplin manufacturing. The department store was built in several stages during the 1850s and was the first of its kind in Dublin, extending over five stories. Pim's managed to survive until the 1970s, when the store was demolished, to be replaced by a mundane office block. Today, right opposite the site of the old store, there's a restaurant and bar called, appropriately, J. T. Pim's.

Quinnsworth

The first Quinnsworth supermarket was opened in the brand new Stillorgan shopping centre at the end of 1966, by Pat Quinn. It soon expanded into a nationwide chain of supermarkets that was eventually taken over by Tesco just over 30 years later. In 1997.

Quinnsworth developed a range of its own products, under the Yellow Pack label, which soon became synonymous for something that was cheap and nasty. Even today, 20 years after the Quinnsworth stores were renamed Tesco, the infamous Yellow Pack description still lingers on in public memory.

Ranelagh old shops

Ranelagh is a good example of one of Dublin's "villages" that has changed beyond all recognition in the past 20 years, with the disappearance of all its old shop.

Among the most recent to have closed down was McCarthy's shoe shop, a fixture in Ranelagh for well over 50 years, but which closed down in 2018. Further down that section of the main road in Ranelagh was Dowling's shoe repair shop, almost underneath the Luas bridge. It traded for many years as the place to bring shoes for repair in Ranelagh, but the shop is now derelict. Going along the main road, towards the Triangle, old shops that have gone included Gordon's pharmacy and Pendred's butchers, with the Super Valu supermarket on the site. The supermarket itself has undergone much change, as this used to be a branch of Superquinn. Gilbey's old wine shop gave way to the forecourt of the AIB bank branch. Just past the bank, on the far side of Ranelagh

Avenue, what was once the Lucan Dairy is now the Natural Bakery shop and Diep at Home. The old newsagent's shop on the corner of Westmoreland Park has now been replaced by Lidl. The Spar supermarket, just before the turn into Chelmsford Avenue closed down two years ago and hasn't yet been replaced.

The Spar supermarket in Ranelagh is now on the opposite side of the road, facing the Triangle, and now contains the An Post sub post office. This Spar site was once occupied by Gordon' s, for years, a well- known hardware shop and chandlery. Another hardware shop in Ranelagh was Quinns, which started in the 1940s, when Ranelagh had a total of five hardware shops, and lasted until the 1990s. One of the shops in The Triangle that has long disappeared is Astra Travel, once one of the most popular shops in Ranelagh.

One long renowned shop that has long gone from this part of Ranelagh was McCambridge' s. The firm had started in Shop Street, Galway, in 1925 and it's still going strong there. But in 1945, one of the family, Malcolm McCambridge, came to Dublin and started a shop in Ranelagh, which soon became noted for its brown soda bread and other bread and deli specialities. It lasted for 40 years, until 1985, but the McCambridge bread firm is still going strong, one of the leading bread providers in the Irish market. Gammell's bakery and café subsequently took over, in the same premises.

Travelling out of Ranelagh, in the direction of Sandford Road, one of the big grocery shops, The General Stores, often a chaotic jumble, has been gone for nearly 20 years. Run by the O' Hagan family for around half a century, at 87 Ranelagh, there was also a flower shop at number 83, run by Ann O' Hagan. Both these shops were close to Humphrey's pub, which still retains many of its traditional architectural features. On the far side of The General Stores was Quinn's hardware stores and then what became Kentucky Fried Chicken.

Keighron's newsagent's shop at 73 Ranelagh, just past Humphreys, had traded there since the early 1950s, when Brian Leighron's widowed mother bought the premises, at a time when Ranelagh had 10 newsagents and tobacconists. Brian himself started in the shop as soon as he left school and then ran it for many years until eventually selling it in 2006. The shop became G Male and at the end of 2018, the premises were up for sale.

Brian himself, a a flamboyant character who was one of the mainstays of the old shops in Ranelagh, died in 2015. A little further along that side of Ranelagh, what was once a long established butcher's shop, Kelly Bros, has long since been replaced by one of the village's leading fashion shops, Kelli Fashion.

Just off the main road through Ranelagh, in Chelmsford Avenue, Leary's photographic shop was a mainstay for well over 30 years, but it closed down close on 10 years ago and the premises remained derelict for many years. However, they are now occupied by an art gallery. Also based in Chelmsford Road for many years was the headquarters of the Consumers Association.

One of the most recent "characters" of Ranelagh to pass on was Tony Farmar, whose book publishing firm, A & A Farmar, was long established in the row of houses opposite the Ulster Bank. Tony was one of the best- known and most energetic people in the Irish book publishing trade, but he died in December, 2017.

Rathgar old shops

Bernie Ladd

Rathgar has long had a variety of shops, but many have closed down in recent years. One shop that has long since closed down was Fashion Shoes, owned and run by the O' Connor family. It had been a branch of the old Munster & Leinster Bank, at the start of the Terenure Road, but after it was converted into a shoe shop, the O' Connors lived above the shop. In more recent times, the ground floor of this premises has been the Bottler's Bank pub, next door to the long established Coman's pub.

Another shop that has been long gone was Davis's newsagents shop, where Rathgar Travel is now based. The old newsagent's shop had a great variety of newspapers from Dublin, around the country and abroad, and in the 1960s, used to do a tremendous trade. The owner of the shop also organised the shop in nearby St Luke's hospital for many years after his wife died.

At one stage, Rathgar also had no fewer than four pharmacies, including a branch of Hamilton Long. Another long gone tradesman from the village was Albert Gray, the shoemaker. On the Rathgar Road, a shop called The Sweeties, run by two sisters, appropriately enough, sold a vast array of sweets. Gilbeys the wine merchants also had a shop in Rathgar, while the garage beside the Highfield Stores in now a Super Valu branch. Much more recent shops in Rathgar have also closed down, such as the Gourmet Shop.

It was started in 1968 by brothers Seán and Tommy Cronin, on the site of the old Leverett & Frye grocery shop. The Gourmet Shop became renowned for its selection of exquisite food items; one of its many specialities was honey. Seán Cronin used to produce all his own honey, keeping his beehives beyond Rathfarnham. Seán Cronin, who contributed so much to good food retailing in Rathgar, died in June, 2017. In the 1960s, Rathgar had other food shops, such as McCabe's fish shop, and a sweet shop called Miss Muffett' s.

Rathgar also has yet another claim to fame; for years, it contained the film processing firm that processed all the Agfa film sold in Ireland. Lyall Smith ran for many years at 47 Terenure Road East; Adrienne Bourke worked there for six years.

Rathmines old shops

Michael Lee

Rathmines is still a shopping mecca, but over the past 50 years, its shops have changed out of all recognition.

Neil O' Callaghan, who is now 88, grew up in Leinster Road, close to the Lower Rathmines Road, and remembers vividly all the old shops along the main road and close by.

Barretts was a great toy shop in Castlewood Avenue and sold lots of Hornby train sets. Baggotts was a noted newsagent at the corner of Castlewood Avenue, a newsagent that also sold books, stamps and confectionery. Reads was the radio shop, in the days when everyone depended on their wireless set for news and entertainment. One of the highlights for many people was Ferguson's cake shop and café, where the Swan shopping centre is now located. Ferguson's tea shop was upstairs and there people could be served some of the delicious cakes on sale in the shop. According to Adrienne Bourke, their meringues were killers, one would literally die for them and since their demise, she's never tasted meringues as nice. Close to Ferguson's was Carey's ice cream shop.

Among the butcher's shops in Rathmines, in the days when butchers' shops were separate from pork butchers, was Baby Beef. Pork butchers included Nolans and O' Gormans. Another food shop was the Monument Creameries, noted for its slabs of butter that came in wooden boxes. People often used those boxes for garden sets. Liptons, another grocery chain that's long since gone, had an outlet close to the Stella cinema.

Michael Lee

Rathmines also had quite a selection of sweet shops, including one that was also a tobacconist, at the start of Rathgar Road, remembers Neil, but sadly, they are all long since gone. Bakeries, too, were well represented, such as the Johnston, Mooney and O' Brien cake shop. Neil also remembers that Malachy Quinn started Dublin's first cut price grocery shop on the Upper Rathmines Road. A German style butcher's shop was run by Edward Brenner ar 312 Lower Rathmines Road.

A much more recent closure was Lenehans hardware shop, which shut up shop in 2016, after more than 70 years trading in Rathmines. The building was subsequently turned into a restaurant.

Shaw's was a great hardware shop in the old days, while one of the old drapery, baby wear and ladies' fashions shops was the one run by the Quinn family at 145 Upper Rathmines Road. The family lived above the shop until the 1970s. Liam Quinn remembers that his mother had worked as a drapery buyer in Lee's famous shop before setting up her own business. The old family shop is now Lawlor's the butchers. Another noted ladies fashion shop was Nora Pasley, at 204 Lower Rathmines Road.

In the old days, the biggest shop in Rathmines was Lees, which was on the main road just after the turn for Castlewood Avenue. It sold everything from fashions to bedding, carpets and curtains, everything for the house. Michael Lee remembers that the greatest fun he and his siblings had when they were children was watching cash being put into small metal and wood containers, then loaded into an overhead pulley system. The canisters were shot at great speed in the direction of the cash office and the change came back the same way. Another fond memory is of the staff stretching felt hats on a wooden head shaped block ; it had a large metal screw device that turned to stretch the hats. The three floors of Lee's department store were full of delights, especially at Christmas time, when they were packed with toys.

Michael Lee

Beside Lees, on the Castlewood Avenue side, was Hamilton Long, the chemists, while on the other side was the ESB showrooms. Three shops beyond the ESB outlet was an outlet for Findlaters, the old grocery and wine firm. Before the ESB shop was built, an old fashioned grocery shop called Dwyers was next to Lees.

Another striking shop in the old days in Rathmines was the shop run by P. Ryan & Sons, on the Lower Rathmines Road, directly across the road from the old Princess cinema. Ryan's sold everything electrical, as well as radios, cycles and prams. The shop was extensively renovated and included a spacious workshop at the rear. After the renovation, Ryan's was in many ways the most modern looking shop in Rathmines, but it closed down in the early 1960s. Some of its neon lighting adorned Kelly's electrical shop in Ranelagh until the late 1970s.

Yet another renowned shop in Rathmines that closed down 20 years ago was the Blindcraft shop on Lower Rathmines Road, where baskets and other goods made by blind people were sold. The

Blindcraft factory in Dublin had been set up in 1957 and for many years, its workers, people with no sight or else poor vision, made high quality bedding, furniture and toiletries. The Rathmines shop was the outlet for these goods for many years before being transferred to Inchicore and the government decided in 2004 to consign the organisation to the scrapheap, as one of its workers put it.

Martin Ryan

Reads, Parliament Street

Reads was the oldest shop in Dublin, founded in 1675 at Blind Quay. But in 1750, it moved to Parliament Street, with a rear entrance onto Crane Street. The founder of the shop was James Read, whose sister gave birth to Arthur Guinness, the founder of the famous brewery. For many decades, Reads sold all manner of items forged from metal, everything from cutlery to swords. In 1988, Jack Cowle, the last descendent of the Reads, died and the shop was taken over by the Butler family, who ran it until 1997. In recent years, the shop and the building it's in have been fully restored and in October, 2018, the premises were put up for sale with a price tag of €2. 5 million.

Richard & Alan, Grafton Street

Before the second world war, Jack Clarke had run a substantial drapery manufacturing business, and opened his shop in Grafton Street, named after his two sons, and designed to keep his wealthier clients in touch with the latest fashion trends. At one stage, Jack Clarke's was the top clothing exporter in Ireland, employing over 300 people at its peak. The Grafton Street shop, at numbers 57 and 58, became one of the top retail fashion outlets in the street after it opened in 1936. But in 2012, it moved into the lower ground floor at Pamela Scott's fashion shop at 84 Grafton Street.

Other well- known retailers on the street, except for men, were F. X. Kelly and Tyson' s, all gone, along with the Banba bookshop, close to where Dubray Books now has its Grafton Street shop.

Road Records, Fade Street

Road Records was at 16B Fade Street and was run by Dave Kennedy and Jackie Collins. It closed in late 2010 after 11 years in business and was replaced by the R. A. G. E. shop selling retro consoles and games. Road Records had been noted for selling music records that were hard to find elsewhere and one of the well-known performers who visited it regularly was Glen Hasard.

RTV Rentals

After Telefis Éireann started Ireland's first television station in 1962, later to become RTÉ, a number of firms sprung up to rent TV sets to customers. The leading firm was RTV Rentals, which had many shops not only in Dublin but in towns and cities across the country. Its Dublin branches included 40 Upper Baggot Street, which eventually became Baggot Print & Design. It's now a Mexican fast food restaurant. RTV Rentals lasted until 2006, when Joe Fitzgerald, the managing director, decided to retire and the last three branches, one in Dublin, one in Waterford and one in Wexford were closed. The business faded away as it became cheaper for customers to buy their sets.

Another business that faded rapidly was Xtravision, which rented out videos, but its market shrank as it became much easier to download films. Its extensive network included a large store at the corner of Waterloo Road and Upper Baggot Street, Dublin, which is now an estate agents. The most drastic closure of the Xtravision network came in 2015, when it decided to close down 28 of its shops nationwide.

South Anne Street post office

An Post museum and archive

For many years, South Anne Street had an extensive post office, which opened in 1954. It was renovated on two occasions, in 1966 and 1988. After that last renovation, it started providing a bilingual service in Irish and English for its customers, but it closed down on April 30, 2004. The premises is now occupied by T. M. Lewin, a men's outfitters based in Jermyn Street, London.

St Stephen's Green

One retailer, long gone, but still much missed, was Smith's on the Green, at the Grafton Street end of the Green. It was a renowned, high class provisions' shop that had an amazing selection of often foreign produced food items that in the 1960s and 1970s, were almost impossible to buy anywhere else in Dublin.

Stein's opticians, Harcourt Road

Dublin born Mendel Stein, born in 1915 and brought up in Victoria Street, Portobello, which was then part of a strong Jewish community in the area, qualified as an ophthalmic optician. He opened his own shop at 36 Harcourt Road in 1944. Known as "The Eye", it became one of the most popular opticians in the city and Mendel became close friends with many in the theatrical and artistic community in Dublin. All was going well until 1983, when a development company announced plans for a seven storey office block, which became the Harcourt Centre. Mendel said he wouldn't leave until the developers gave him a new shop in the immediate vicinity, with the window of the shopfront in the shape of an eye.

He held out so long that his shop was the only surviving remnant of the old shops along this part of Harcourt Road, while the new office block was being built all round it. On one occasion, a quick witted young Dubliner shouted in to Mendel: "hey, mister, your extension is coming on great". In time, the shop was taken down and re- erected in nearby Grantham Street, where Mendel was joined by huis daughter Amelia. Mendel died in June, 2000.

Suffolk Street

Among the long vanished retailers in this street were Walpole's linen shop and Gibson Price, men's outfitters, together with the Indian Tea shop.

Switzers

Switzers was once one of the two top department stores in Grafton Street, the other being Brown Thomas, just opposite, on the other side of the street. Switzers dated back to 1838, when it started as a drapery store. Towards the end of the 19th century, the firm acquired buildings at the corner of Grafton Street and Wicklow Street, as well as in Clarendon Street, that enabled it to develop a department store.

In 1960, Switzers became associated with Cash's of Cork, which also brought them into Galway and Limerick. But just over a decade later, in 1971, Switzers itself was taken over hy the House of Fraser and Waterford Glass. Then in 1995, it was acquired by Brown Thomas, which moved out of its own store, handing it over to Marks & Spencer. The old Switzers name vanished in favour of Brown Thomas, which is still trading, very successfully, on the same site today.

Templeogue

In Templeogue village, there used to be a lovely little shop and sub post office run by Margaret and Pat Troy, recalls Eithne MeKeon. They were right beside the AIB bank branch and although long closed, the Troys' shops are sorely missed. Eithne says that it was such a nice friendly village shop.

Terenure old shops

Richard William Heaney

The most important "vanished shop in Terenure, according to Jimmy Doyle, who has long connections with the area, and also John Bryan Allen, was Floods, the big conglomeration of shops in the area in the 1950s and 1960s. According to Jimmy, Floods included everything from a grocery shop, where most of the produce was sold loose, to a fish shop, a vegetable and fruit shop, a chemist's and even a pub. Floods closed in 1970, after 70 years' trading and the premises is now occupied by Brady's pub. Close by is another historic Terenure pub, Vaughan' s.

Other shops that have long vanished from Terenure include Imco dry cleaners, Prescott Cleaners, Eastman's the butchers and RTV, the television rental shop. What was the Home Stores, a hardware store run by the Lamont family, is now an estate agents, Quillsens. Fine's jewellers shop did a good business people after many Jewish people moved to the area from the South Circular Road area, but that too has now gone. The Classic Cinema close to the crossroads in Terenure, which had opened in 1938, lasted until 1976; it was converted into a business centre. Just opposite the Classic were the old offices of the Sunday World newspaper, which has also long departed Terenure and is now based in the headquarters of Independent News & Media in Talbot Street.

According to Jimmy, only one shop that traded in Terenure in the old days when Terenure really was a village, is Roche's barber' shop, run by the same family who started it in the 1950s. Two shops that closed down in 2018 were both family owned, O' Toole's butchers and Downey's butchers. O' Toole's was on the site of the old Eastman's butcher's shop and when that chain of shops stopped trading, Jimmy O' Toole, the manager of its Terenure branch, started his own shop on the same site.

Another recent closure was of Rathdown Motors, which shut at Christmas, 2012, with the loss of 18 jobs. As Jimmy Doyle says, of all the shops in Terenure that were listed in the 1960 edition of Thom's Directory, every single one has long since gone. One of the general grocery shops that has long since vanished is Heaneys, at 22 Terenure Road North, which prided itself on selling just one quality of goods, the best. It sold groceries, provisions, confectionery, cigarettes and dairy products and was run by the parents of Richard William Heaney who still lives in Terenure. His parents were Winifred and William, so W. Heaney was a very appropriate name for the shop. The shop operated from 1942 until 1983 and today, the site is part of the Tesco car park on Terenure

Road North. The biggest retail outlet today in Terenure is the huge Aldi store.

Today, many of the old shops in Terenure have been replaced by restaurants, with the area now having a dozen, a similar trend to what's happened in many other suburban areas of Dublin, like Ranelagh or Sandymount.

Thomas Street

Thomas Street in the 1960s had a great variety of shops, both locally owned and part of nationwide chains, but all have long since gone.

Seezer's pork butchers traded here from 1900 for a century; a sign in the window said that Charles Seezer, the owner, was a "humane killer". Annie Craddock, a haberdasher, was renowned for buttons and other drapery essentials. Millars had a branch here, selling everything from tea to wine and whiskey, while the renowned Findlater's chain had a grocery and wine shop in the street, along with Eastman's the butchers. Other locally owned shops included Sheppard's Dairy, while Foley's chemist's shop had a display in its front window that was called Mushatt's natural medicines. It was dedicated to Harold Mushatt, a "kill or cure cure" chemist, who originally started business in Francis Street before being taken over by Foley's in Thomas Street. That feature in Foley's window survived for over 40 years.

Another long gone traditional shop very close to Thomas Street was Halton's grocery shop in Francis Street, renowned for its weighing scales and bacon slicer, which would now be considered very archaic.

Todd Burns, Mary Street

For many years, Todd Burns was a department store in Mary Street. Construction had started in 1902 and the façade was built with red brick and terracotta detail. The building also featured a large bronze dome. The Volta Cinema, run by James Joyce, had stood on the site. Todd Burns had been controlled by the Revington family of Tralee, Co Kerry, but in 1969, Galen Weston became a director. Todd Burns was soon taken over and Penney's opened its first store here that same year.

Penneys expanded very quickly; within two years, it had 12 stores in the Republic and 11 in Northern Ireland. Today, it has some 250 stores in close to a dozen countries, but its headquarters remains in Mary Street, where the old building, once the Todd Burns store, was completely renovated in 2013.

Turnover tax

This tax, introduced by a Fianna Fáil government in 1963, sounded the death knell for many small shops, just as larger supermarkets were starting to gear up. Many protests took place, including a monster meeting of over 3, 000 small traders, at the Mansion House on Dublin's Dawson Street. That happened in early May, 1963, while in July of that year, over 10, 000 small traders from all over the State marched through Dublin.

The protests by traders and organisations like RGDATA were to no avail; the government refused to make any concessions, except one, that the hated new tax would be levied at the rate of five shillings for the first £100 of turnover. The new retail tax came into effect on November 1,1963, then wholesale tax came in during 1966. These two taxes were the predecessors of VAT, which was introduced in 1972, in preparation for Ireland joining the then EEC, on January 1, 1973. But in the previous decade, the hated turnover tax had done its deadly work of largely destroying Ireland's small shops.

Upper Baggot Street

Parson's bookshop just before it closed

Frank Fennell

Two very traditional businesses on Baggot Street Bridge have long since closed. The former branch of the Bank of Ireland closed down a decade ago and is now a branch of the Milano's restaurant chain. An even bigger loss was that of Parson's bookshop, which traded from 1949 until 1989.

Owned by May O' Flaherty, who was assisted by Mary King and three other ladies, the shop was a keystone of what was then the bohemian district of this part of Dublin 4, known as Baggotonia. Brendan Behan and Patrick Kavanagh often visited the shop, although they took good care never to be there at the same time, since they were deadly enemies. Frank O' Connor and Mary Lavin, both of whom lived nearby, also visited, as did Flann O' Brien and in more recent times, Seamus Heaney. Well- known artists, such as John Behan and Patrick Pye, also enjoyed the unique atmosphere of Parson's Bookshop.

After the shop closed down in 1989, it went through a variety of uses, including as a newagents and as a deli. Its most reincarnation has been as a branch of FBD Insurance, a far cry from the old Baggotonia, which has long since vanished.

The picture of retail shops in Upper Baggot Street in the 1960s has changed so drastically that today, only five of the retail outlets that were there then are still trading today. The Wellington Bar, at the corner of the street and Mespil Road, is still trading after 135 years. The Kylemore Bakery long had a bakery shop at Number 9, while another shop that's long gone was Dowling's butchers at Number 11; these days, butcher's shops are amongst the most endangered. After Dowling's, Murphy's newsagents traded for many years until it was taken over by Donnybrook Fair in 2004. The Mercury travel agency at Number 15 is long gone, since most travel bookings these days are done online. Also long vanished is the Farm Produce shop at Number 17. Kilmartin's was a very successful bistro type restaurant at Number 19, name after the bookie's shop that had previously traded at the same address. The restaurant ran from 1979 until 1993.

Weir's hardware shop, at Number 21, dates back to 1885, but during a hiatus in the 1960s, Five Star supermarkets traded there.

But the Left Bank Boutique at Number 31A is long vanished. Gone even longer is the board for blind employment, which once stood at the corner of Upper Baggot Street and Waterloo Road and provided work for blind people, making baskets.

On the other side of Upper Baggot Street, starting at the Haddington Road corner, Mooney's pub, part of a long vanished chain of pubs in Dublin, closed down 35 years ago and was replaced by a branch of Permanent TSN bank. Lipton's grocery shop at Number 4 is long gone, as is Dunn's fish and deli shop at Number 6 and Eastman's butcher's at Number 12. But in this particular part of the street, Meagher's chemists, founded in 1929, is still going strong, as is the other pharmacy, Boots, situated where Hayes Conyngham and Robinson once had a chemist's shop.

At Number 20, Open Till Eight, renowned for its trendy ladies fashions, was one of the most popular shopping destinations on the street in the 1960s. Almost next door, the old Findlater's grocery store has long since given way to Tesco, while at Number 40, RTV, a television rental shop, had its heyday in the 1960s. It subsequently became Baggot Print & Design and the premises is now Tolteca, a Mexican café and takeway. The Waterloo Bar is very long established, dating back to 1840, while Searson's bar goes back to about 1860. In more recent times, the Koinop launderette stood next to Searson' s, but that too has long since passed into history, along with the branch of the Monument Creamery and an outlet for Blanchardstown Mills.

Verschoyle Place/ Lower Mount Street

the old Shoe Hospital in Grattan Street

Des Kerins

Andy Jones, who grew up in this area, remembers that as a child, in Verschoyle Place, there were several shops, including Bannon's grocery and dairy, at the Merrion Square end. Mrs Bannon, a tall, elegant lady with a very posh accent, sold all kinds of groceries. The shop was full of large sacks of flour, sugar, rice and other "loose" foodstuffs, which were scooped out into blue paper bags. On the back counter, there was a large block of butter, from which sections were sliced off to order. The wooden paddles used were kept in a jug of water. Andy also remembers being sent to the shop to buy a 2d "Mac's Smiles" razor blade for his dad's Sunday morning shave.

Also nearby were two small shops, one selling sweets, the others a shoe repairers, while there was also Maggie Mitchell's grocery shop.

In Power's Court, a tiny shop was owned and run by a large, jolly woman called May Heffernan. She smiled a lot, but spoke little. Andy remembers the combination of smells in the shop, paraffin and aniseed balls. Another nearby shop was Tracey' s, which faced onto a cleared area that was used for football. This particular area also had a notorious pub, known as "the Hive".

On Lower Mount Street, Andy remembers that there were many shops. His favourites included Bob Moult' s, near the bridge over the Grand Canal. It was a newsagents and tobacconists and Andy often read Dublin Opinion there. At the maternity hospital end of the street, a very upmarket tobacco shop was called, appropriately enough, The Elite.

Another great favourite was the shop run by Mrs Ennis, halfway along Lower Mount Street. Andy says it was a strange place to have a grocery shop. Customers went up the high double sided steps from the street and the shop was in the front downstairs room, which presumably had once been someone's drawing room.

Andy says that despite all the disadvantages of the time, 60 and more years ago, including gas lighting, outside lavatories and rampant TB, there was a joie de vivre about the area. People had little, but what they had, they shared. "We were surrounded by relations, lived in each other's houses or rooms and we enjoyed our childhood", he says. So strong was the pull of the area that after Andy's family moved to Ballyfermot, for several years, his mother still travelled all the way in to do her shopping at the shop run by

Mrs Ennis. But as Andy concludes, "when I make my once a year visit to the area now, I feel sad".

Village News, Sandymount

For about 15 years at the end of the 20th century, Vincent Tierney and his wife ran this local newsagents and post office. In 2002, they decided to retire from the business and the Village News closed down. The shop has since been replaced by modern buildings, including a pub and a restaurant.

Walton's music shop, North Frederick Street

Martin Walton, a violinist and freedom fighter in the War of Independence (1919- 1921), opened his first shop, in North Frederick Street, in 1922. For many years, it was famed for its sheet music and instruments, but closed in 2013. Walton also founded the Dublin School of Music in 1924. A second shop was opened at South Great George's Street in 1992 and this lasted until 2018, leaving Walton's with just one shop, in the Blanchardstown shopping centre.

For over 30 years, Walton's had a Saturday lunchtime radio show on what became Radio 1, compered by Leo Maguire. He also wrote many songs, including the Dublin Saunter, for his friend, Noel Purcell. The show lasted until 1980, shortly before RTÉ stopped broadcasting sponsored shows. For many years, the best-known catchphrase for the programme had been "if you sing a song, do sing an Irish song".

Waterstone's bookshop, Dawson Street

Waterstone's old bookshop on Dawson Street traded there for the best part of 10 years, a unique emporium of books on two floors. But it and the Waterstone's branch in the Jervis shopping centre both closed down in 2011. The shop in Dawson Street remained vacant for three years until Tower Records moved in, after spending 21 years in Wicklow Street.

Wee Stores, Pembroke Lane

The Wee Stores opened in 1920 in a converted coach house in Pembroke Lane, rendered redundant by the arrival of motor cars in the first two decades of the 20th century. In 1941, it was taken over by John Harrison, who had other shops in Dublin, at North King Street and near the Four Courts. He and his wife Catherine ran the shop for many years and its wide range of grocery items, as well as coal and peat briquettes, were very much in demand by local residents. One very popular item was pipe cleaners, used by women for doing their hair, while in the run up to Christmas, red candles were very popular.

But the arrival of the first supermarkets in nearby Upper Baggot Street in the early 1960s, together with the introduction of turnover tax, hit small shops like the Wee Stores badly and trade never recovered. After the deaths of John Harrison and his wife, the shop was let to a variety of other retailers, including Sheridan's the esteemed cheesemongers and a French- owned jewellery and fashion shop, but for nearly 10 years now, the premises have been occupied by First Editions, an antiquarian book shop run by Allan Gregory, whose wife Carmel is the daughter of the Harrisons.

West' s, jewellers, Grafton Street

While its arch rival, Weirs, at the corner of Grafton Street and Wicklow Street, has kept going steadily, right up to the present day, West' s, on the opposite side of Grafton Street, hasn' t. It closed down in 2010; it had a much longer pedigree than Weir' s, dating back to its foundation in Capel Street in 1720.

Wellington Quay

In the 1960s, the Ireland Benefit Building Society had a branch at Number 27 Wellington Quay, long since vanished, absorbed into the old First National Building Society, itself long disappeared, as have all the other building societies that proliferated until the 1970s. Even workers in the Guinness Brewery had their own building society to fall back on for home loans, but it too was swallowed up by the old First National.

Westmoreland Street

On the right- hand side of this street, facing Nelson's Pillar, the old Irish Times shop was a long time mainstay, but eventually, the corner of Westmoreland Street and Fleet Street was redeveloped for the Educational Building Society.

On the opposite side of the street, Rowan's Seeds, next to the Bank of Ireland, was a popular spot for horticulturalists for many years. Its owner, Fergus Rowan, was a legendary figure, a tireless activist against the big banks, especially Bank of Ireland and AIB. He died in 2008, aged 84. Also on this side of Westmoreland Street were other long gone trading names, including McKenzie's coal, Duffy's bookshop and Battersbys, estate agents and auctioneers.

Woolworth' s, Grafton Street and Henry Street

Willem van de Poll

Woolworth's opened its first Irish store at the top of Grafton Street, on April 23, 1914. For many years, it traded very successfully and the Grafton Street store was substantially rebuilt in the 1960s. Soon after Grafton Street, Woolworth's opened a second Dublin store, in Henry Street. Apart from a vast range of low cost merchandise, the Woolworth's stores were also noted for their cafés, perennial favourites especially with children. But in 1984, all the Woolworth's stores in Ireland closed, four years before the chain shut in the UK.

OLD THEATRES

Andrews Lane Theatre

This theatre, which was situated between Trinity Street and Exchequer Street, just off Dame Street, opened in 1989 and managed to stay open until 2007. The small theatre put on some memorable productions, including premieres for works by the likes of Roddy Doyle, Brien Friel and Maeve Binchy. After it closed, it was turned into a nightclub. But all trace of the old theatre will soon vanish, as planning permission has been given for the demolition of the old building and its replacement by a €21 million, 136 bedroom hotel.

Archbishop Byrne Hall, Harrington Street

Also known as St Kevin's Hall, it was long used for amateur productions and today, it's still being used for dancing classes.

Bewley's café- theatre, Grafton Street

The theatre at Bewley's in Grafton Street opened in 1999, for lunchtime theatre. Following the extensive renovations of Bewley's, the theatre reopened in 2018.

Damer Hall, St Stephen's Green

For many years, especially in the 1950s and 1960s, this was a popular theatrical venue, beside the Unitarian church. The downstairs Damer Theatre was often used for Irish language productions and Behan's play, An Giall (The Hostage) was premiered there.

Eblana Theatre

The Eblana Theatre ran in the basement of Busarus in 1959 and managed to survive until 1955. Its guiding light for many years was Phyllis Ryan, who put on many memorable and often experimental productions in the small theatre.

Focus Theatre, off Upper Fitzwilliam Street

This innovative theatre, which also trained actors and directors in the use of the Stanislavski system, was started on 1963 by Deirdre O' Connell, an Irish- American actor who was married to Luke Kelly of The Dubliners. Many prominent actors were associated with the Focus Theatre, including Gabriel Byrne, Sabina Coyne (wife of President Michael D. Higgins), Tom Hickey and Bosco Hogan. The theatre was small and survived for many years without any State subsidies, staging nearly 400 productions altogether, usually very innovative. It closed in 2012, 11 years after the death of Deirdre O' Connell.

Garrick Theatre, 15 Parnell Square

This theatre and Studio 8 were well- known places for theatrical performances; the Gate Theatre continues that tradition today, along with Theatre 36. Substantial plans have been announced to create the Parnell Square Cultural Quarter, including a massive new city council library.

Gas Company theatres, D' Olier Street and Dún Laoghaire

The old Dublin Gas company had two theatres, one in D' Olier Street, the other in Dún Laoghaire and up to the 1970s, both were widely used. The Gas Company building in D' Olier Street was particularly distinctive, built in 1928 in the Art Deco style.

Overend Hall, St John Ambulance, Upper Leeson Street

The hall was built at the back of the St John Ambulance headquarters in 1957 and for many years, it was used for many purposes, including musical performances. For many years, RTÉ used the hall for orchestral rehearsals, but these days, it's main use is for exams set by various outside organisations.

John Player Theatre, South Circular Road

This one time manufacturing complex was built for a cigarette company in 1935 and for many years, the theatre was a popular venue. The building now awaits redevelopment.

Jury's Hotel, Ballsbridge

The cabaret at Jury's Hotel in Ballsbridge was legendary for decades. But the hotel is now known as the Ballsbridge Hotel and is slated for redevelopment.

Lantern Theatre, 38 Merrion Square

The Lantern Theatre Club was active here from 1957 until 1975.

Oscar Theatre, Serpentine Avenue, Sandymount

A former cinema, this became a theatre in the mid- 1970s and lasted for just over a decade, until it closed in 1986. It was renowned for putting on the first all- nude stage show in Dublin, in a bid to revive its flagging fortunes.

Pike Theatre, Herbert Lane

The Pike Theatre was a small theatre started by Carolyn Swift, a noted actor, writer and critic and her husband Alan Simpson, another leading theatrical personality in 1953. It lasted for 11 years, until 1964. In 1957, the Pike Theatre staged the Rose Tattoo by Tennessee Williams and during a performance, it appeared that a condom was dropped on the stage. Subsequently, the State unsuccessfully tried to bring a prosecution for obscenity, but the sensation reverberated for years afterwards. The fact that the Pike Theatre had put on works by the likes of Brendan Behan and Samuel Beckett became overshadowed by a controversy that to modern eyes seems utterly ridiculous.

Queen's Theatre, Pearse Street

The Queen's Theatre in Pearse Street was a Victorian building that managed to survived until the end of the 1960s. It had a traditional style audiotorium. After the Abbey Theatre was destroyed by fire in 1951, it moved to the Queen's Theatre and stayed there until the new Abbey Theatre, the present construction, opened in 1966. After the Abbey moved back to its traditional base, the Queen's Theatre remained empty until it was demolished in 1969. As has happened so often in Dublin, this venerable theatre was replaced by a soulless modern office building.

Rupert Guinness Hall, St James's Street

A well- known performance venue for many years, close to the Guinness brewery, it's still in existence.

St Anthony's Theatre, Merchant's Quay

This theatre was particularly known for its pantomimes during the 1990s.

Studio Theatre Club, 43 Upper Mount Street

This was one of a number of small theatre clubs, often in basements, that were popular in the Dublin of the 1950s and 1960s.

Theatre Royal, Hawkins Street

Dublin had a total of five Theatre Royals. The fifth and final version opened in 1935, designed as both a theatre and a cinema. The auditorium was huge, holding 3, 500 patrons seated and a further 300 standing. Many famous national and international players appeared there, including such Irish stars as Patricia Cahill, Paddy Crosbie, Jack Cruise, Noel Purcell and Micheál MacLiammoir, while it also had a renowned troupe of dancers, the Royalettes. The Theatre Royal closed down on June 30, 1962 and subsequently, a hideous office block, Hawkins House, was built on the site. For many years, until 2018, it housed the Department of Health, which has now moved to the former headquarters of the Bank of Ireland on Lower Baggot Street. Hawkins House is now slated for redevelopment.

37 Theatre, 36 Lower Baggot Street

The 37 Theatre was active here in the 1960s; it was co-founded by Barry Cassin, a well- known actor, and Nora Lever.

Tivoli Theatre, Francis Street

The Tivoli was a successor to an earlier Tivoli Theatre, on Burgh Quay, which closed down in 1928 and was then converted into the headquarters of the Irish Press newspaper. The new Tivoli opened in 1934 as a ciné-variety theatre, then in the late 1930s, was converted into a proper cinema, which lasted until 1964.

It was reopened as a live theatre in 1987, but in April, 2019, the building was demolished to make way for a 289 bedroom aparthotel development, which is also due to include a cinema space. Before demolition, the developer had been ordered to make a photographic record of all the graffiti on the site, for the Dublin City Council library service.

FURTHER READING

Ballsbridge Then & Now, Hugh Oram, Dublin, 2012

Castleknock, memories of a neighbourhood, Tony Reynolds, Dublin, 2017

Deeds not words, the life and work of Muriel Gahan, Dublin, 1997

Dublin Churches, Peter Costelloe, Dublin, 1989

Dundrum Then & Now, Hugh Oram, Dublin 2015

Edward Lee, model employer and man of moral courage, Michael Lee, Dún Laoghaire- Rathdown, 2016

Findlaters, the story of a Dublin merchant family, 1774- 2001, Alex Findlater, Dublin, 2001

High Shelves and Long Counters, stories of Irish shops, Heike Thiele, Dublin, 2012

Leeson Street, upper and lower, Hugh Oram, US, 2018

Lost Dublin, Frederick O' Dwyer, Dublin, 1981

Parson's bookshop, at the heart of Bohemian Dublin, 1949- 1989, Brendan Lynch, Dublin, 2006

Sandymount, Hugh Oram, Dublin 2016

S' wonderful, a musical life, by Kevin Hough, Dublin, 2017

Stillorgan in Old Photographs, Hugh Oram, Dublin, 2019

Talking Shop 50 years of the Irish grocery trade, 1942- 1992, Dublin, 1992

The Little Book of Ballsbridge, Hugh Oram, Dublin, 2014

The Little Book of Blackrock, Hugh Oram, Dublin, 2019

The Little Book of Dundrum, Hugh Oram, Dublin, 2014

The Little Book of Merrion and Booterstown, Hugh Oram, Dublin, 2018

The Little Book of Stillorgan, Hugh Oram, Dublin, 2017

Thom's directories (annual), Dublin

When the shopping was good: Woolworths and the Irish main street, Barbara Walsh, Dublin, 2011

ends

Printed in Great Britain
by Amazon